THE PORTLAND EIGHT MILE

# THE
# PORTLAND
# EIGHT
# MILE

## GENE GREGORITS

## MONASTRELL
### 2013

**THE PORTLAND EIGHT MILE**
© 2014  by Justin Gene Gregorits

First published as Monastrell 007 in August 2013.

Manufactured in the United States of America.

Published for Monastrell Books by Gene Gregorits, PO BOX 661, Madeira Beach, FL 33708.

FIRST PRINTING, June 2014.

Book design: Gene Gregorits
Photos by K. Kucharski

Special thanks to Valerie Kilgore

INTRODUCTION:

  My plane made a rather bumpy landing, which had me punching
the air, at approximately 9 A.M., EST. I was now officially
delivered from the smoking remains of an extended booze freakout
that seemed karmic in nature, and had left me both enlightened and
sentenced to the void of myself. Clarity isn't always a good thing.
  Stepping into the cold air, I flinched at every sudden movement or
sound. My boots were caked in tomato juice from the three Bloody
Marys I'd spilled on them during the flight. Upon noticing the red
cesspool around me, the flight attendant had refused to serve me
again. I stated that if she could provide me with a straw long enough
to reach my head, I would not spill a fourth. She'd shaken her head
in disgust, and threatened to report me to the authorities.
  I asked a yuppie cocksucker for a quarter, to help get me from
Philadelphia International to the downtown Greyhound depot. He
told me to get lost.
  I asked another yuppie cocksucker *how* to get from Philadelphia
International airport to the downtown Greyhound depot. He
instructed me to ask someone else.
  Six hours later, my toe broken, and with a look in my eyes that
would make grown men vomit, I had frightened enough change out
of other travelers to get the downtown train. I myself was frightened
too…there was within me enough unbearable dread to murder at
least a dozen Gene Suicides. For six days now, I'd been committing
relentless acts of obliterated obscenity upon myself and others,
ruining a very passionate romance less than 24 hours after it's
official beginning and gutpunching Super Frida for absolutely no
reason at all. I was deranged, repulsively infantile, even by my

standards. I decided that I did not want to make it though the week. I'd committed the most ungodly affront of my entire life and my mask of shame was too ghoulish for anyone to look at, least of all me. Out of some distorted sense of self-preservation, shortly after being dumped drunk out onto the unfamiliar streets of Portland at 9 A.M., I sat in a soup kitchen with grimacing tramps and plotted my motive for survival: a scandalous cry from heaven and a roaring belch from Hell, carried out in the bowels of the most wonderful city I've yet visited, and also the most horrible. I'd write a combination bar crawl report, travel diary, interview anthology, and hardcore apology. I decided to call it, "Going Down on Groundhog Day", before finally deciding on:

# THE PORTLAND EIGHT MILE

A Northwestern Nightmare Odyssey

By Gene Gregorits, Pecker on a Downward Spiral
with Miss Satanica T. Szandor

"There has rarely in this world been a more irredeemable open wound of a man than Gene Gregorits."
-Thomas Ignatius Preston III

"Fuck you, I just got fisted."
-Miss Satanica

"Sodom and Gomorrah, they run the roadhouse."
-John Cougar

"If you know, don't let me go."
-Shane MacGowan

"This is the North, lad. Up here, we do what we want."
-David Peace

# FEBRUARY 7, 2003

Appx. 11 AM

Upon arrival at the Philadelphia Greyhound depot, I use my very
last $15 to purchase a ticket on the 2:16 to Harrisburg. Finally, after
six days of no sleep, no sanity, and no clean socks, I collapse
halfway up the short staircase on the West entrance. Before I knew
I'd fallen, two black cabbies rushed over and peered at me through
the dingy sunlight, saying through broken yellow teeth,

"Hey man! You alright?"

"N-n-no."

"You need a cab?"

"Yeah. B-b-but I don't have any money."

"What's wrong with you?"

"Everything."

"Get outta here." He looks at his homey, and says, "fuckin white
boy crazy."

"I'm having DTs. I've been drunk straight through for nearly six
months. And now, I can't make it home."

"Where home?"

"Philadelphia."

"Yo man, you *is* in Philly!"

"Harrisburg."

"Sheee-it."

"Look, I have six very expensive VCRs. Together, they're worth
nearly two thousand dollars. Thing is, I already have my bus ticket,
but it doesn't leave for another hour. And I can't make it. Drive me
home and I'll give you all six fucking VCRs."

"Uh…"

"They're really good machines. They're worth three grand."

"You just said two."

"I meant three."

" I don't know, man. I need money, not VCRs."

"Well, thanks anyway."

"Yo Bill! This guy say he got six VCRs."

8

Bill looks up like I have Jack the fucking Ripper standing behind me.

"Say they worth three grand. Need to go to Harrisburg."

A small crowd has gathered. I'm going into convulsions, while coughing up chunks of my blackened lungs.

Bill says, "Jesus Christ, man!"

A thick spool of brown tar droops from the back of my throat and I'm hanging onto a parking meter with one hand. I limp off down the street, as fast as I can, a gutted scarecrow.

# FEBRUARY 6, 2003
APPX. 11:30 AM
DRAG QUEEN BAR
## Jimmy, Alaskan fisherman

JIMMY: No. It seems weird, but no one touches this lighter but me. It was a gift from my father. No one uses this lighter but me.

GG: Every time I light a match, a spark flies off the fucker and goes straight for my nose, or my lips.

JIMMY: HAHAHA

GG: See what happened to my lip?

JIMMY: Yeah

GG: So you know. I don't need any more damage. This is fucking dangerous. That's why I need your lighter.

JIMMY: My father gave it to me.

GG: I'm not going anywhere with it! I've got a mini VietNam happening here. I know the next spark is coming straight for my motherfucking eyeball! Help me, don't make me use these on myself.

JIMMY: HAHAHA. Take the fucking lighter, christ!

# FEBRUARY 5, 2003

GG: Can I interview you?

MOTEL BARMAID: No. And you have to stop bothering our guests.

GG: Pardon me for saying so, miss but-

MB: Turn that off.

GG: Okay. But your guests have been bothering *me*. Trying to sell me drugs.

MB: I don't want to hear about that. If you're going to sit here, you have to order something.

GG: How's the food?

MB: What do you want?

GG: Vodka tonic.

TAPE CUTS

GG: I apologize to telemarketers when they wake me up at seven in godforsaken morning of the godforsaken day of the godforsaken night. I'm pathetic. I'm hearing voices and my room stinks worse than anything I've ever smelled. Remember to note that you bought cocaine last night and it turned out to be sugar and laxative and nothing else.

I enjoy your company one minute, and would be quite happy to never see you again the next. A bloody idiot, I suppose, and idiots are the easiest targets. Being the kind of person that you probably are, and to avoid your target practice, I have resigned myself to situations like this one…at least this dumpy black whore, reeking of a cheap, 3 day old musk application, is telling me the truth. And the truth comes with a price. I'm forty bucks shy.

GERALDINE, black whore

(microphone in coat pocket)

GERALDINE: Did you not just hear me say that to her?
GG: Yeah, I heard. Is that guy over there your brother?
G: Yeah.
GG: He's coming back in? He said he was going have a drink with me.
G: He comin.
GG: What did you say your name was?
G: Geraldine.
GG: I'm Gene.
G: Wanna date?
GG: Yeah.
G: What do ya want?
GG: Well the thing is, I only have ten dollars.
G: Sheeeit. Ten bucks won't even get you in my door.
GG: Well, how much then?
G: Everything starts at $50.
GG:  You watching that TV?
G:  Nope.
GG: I want to hear some music.
G: I don't care.

   I spend a buck on three Petty tunes, hit a few more Vodka tonics, split. Frida swings by with breakfast. Hash browns, scrambled eggs, a bagel with tomato and cream cheese. Despite my hunger, I would regret there not being ketchup for my eggs had Frida not brought me ketchup for my eggs. I wolf everything down with Coors, while talking to Frida. Since my blood is infected with cheap yeast, I skip the bagel, but eat the tomatoes and lick the cream cheese off. Frida ignores this, because she is such a fucking saint of a man that I want to kiss her.

# SUPER FRIDA, Cartoonist
Pizza joint, appx. noon

GG: In your cartoon of Jared and Clara and Clay, what I think is great is that you have a political thought commentary going on, about Subway Sandwiches. It's a great reference to pop culture, a statement and a piss take at the same time. It's looking at what is going on in junk food culture today. Another thing that really stands out in that cartoon is your own personal, idiosyncratic *Frida syntax*, as it were…which is the sign, behind Clay, who is buttfucking Jared. SUPER FRIDA: "SUBWAY / THE ENTRANCE IS ALSO AN EXIT."

GG: HAHAHA! You have also reminded me a few times that the top is also the bottom. SF: Transference of power. Exactly. Just a teeter totter! Tit for tat! I got the tat if you got the tit, so…

GG: In Portland, I get more sober the more I drink. Here, the bottom is most certainly the top. Okay, now…I've interviewed before, but a few days ago, we'd never actually met. So we're meeting for the first time. I have more questions I have to ask you, whether you want to answer them or not.

SF: It's an affliction, a life sentence. I understand.

GG: You're wearing the lumberjack coat, which is your personal tribute to-

SF: To the lumberjacks, baby! To Big Smokie! And all of his little buddies!

GG: HAHAHAHAHA!

SF: Exactly! Give a hoot! Go pollute!

GG: You're also a very kind, sweet person. Bearing in mind the malevolence which resides in much of your artwork, how do manage to remain so good-natured? Do you feel burdened by having to represent so much vitriol and ugliness in your doodles?

SF: Well, it comes down to my basic belief that internally, most people are capable of being complete *assholes*. Like I was saying earlier, anyone could be capable of the most despicable crimes. It's just a matter of being boxed into a corner for the wrong reason at the wrong time. So if you can understand that everything is essentially, potentially *hideous*…you know, it gets boring. I don't see a position where I need to walk around deformed and contributing, when I could be more upbeat and encouraging. Not to mention that I *have* an outlet. Not everyone has an outlet. If you can shit it out, get it out of the body, into the potty, that in itself is reason enough to be happy.

GG: You must have considered that one way to save people from misery would be to encourage them to be creative?

SF: Oh yeah, big time. I wouldn't necessarily use the word *art*, because "art" represents to me an elitist, bourgeois thing.

GG: Well *fuck them*! I can use that word. Who the fuck do they think they are to ruin a perfectly good word? I'll use it if I want to. If they want to fudge the word "art", then it's up to us to HOSE THAT MOTHERFUCKER DOWN!

SF: Well, also, how many millions of people are there out there who are like, "*oh, I can't do art*" and "*I can't do this.*" Well, BULLSHIT. If you can just find a way to express yourself…fuckin go plant a garden. Write about whatever you want. Draw about whatever you want. Fuckin make some assprints. I think Farrah Fawcett did that fabulous crap, and of course…well, look where it got her. But fuck that. I love Charlie's Angels.

GG: (laughing) It may not in and of itself *solve anything*, but it can encourage you to continue. And to be strong. If you don't have strength, then *you can't do much fighting*. You can't change anything if you're constantly in a state of disrepair, confusion. If you're constantly looking at life through this negative, blurred lens…that in itself as a response is definitely, *definitely* valid. But why not just realize that…you're *part of the masses*! The way you and I feel…I think most people, if they have the fuckin guts to admit it, probably feel the same way! They choose not to because it's easier to just be spoon-fed whatever's on the TV. I don't care so much art, if we're getting into that. Because if we're ever going to be famous, it'll be after we're all long dead anyway, which may not be that much longer, the way things are going.

GG: Would you be shocked if next week, you heard that Portland was getting nuked, and for whatever reason, you couldn't leave town?

SF: I don't know. I'd probably just drive to the epicenter and have a picnic. Wait it out. If it's gonna happen, I'd just as soon *be right there* and get it over with.

GG: Wouldn't you rather be fucking in your last moments?

SF: Well...hopefully I'd have a little notice prior to it. Then I could fill my dance card up accordingly.

GG: (laughing)

SF: In the last moments? If we're dreaming here?

GG: You and me, we're always dreaming. That's what makes us such freaks. Some people can't afford to dream. We can't buy lunch a lot of the time, but we can dream.

SF: It rains all the time in Portland, so I'm *wet* dreaming too, but that's okay.

GG: (laughing)

SF: If it came down to the last bitter moments, when the blade drops? (pauses) I guess I'd be makin a picnic for everybody…because I like to cook. So that'd be it, yeah. But a lot of fucking before then. Hopefully. (impish chuckle)

TAPE CUTS

GG: Could you say that again?

SF: Sure. When you're a kid, you wanna be a movie star, you wanna be famous. I think that anyone with any amount of intelligence, or real sincerity, enough to express themselves one way or another, should understand that fame sucks. I don't fuckin want fame. I don't wanna be famous. I don't want my privacy *raped* by people that I have no interest in. I have a lot of strong opinions, I've very opinionated. And if I pissed someone off with that, I would be willing to defend it. But I have no interest in this whole thing of "oh, look what I'm wearing." The fashion. The reduction of everything that originally might have started politically, then being reduced into some kind of commodity.

GG: That happened with Vivienne Westwood and the Sex Pistols, didn't it?

SF: Punk rock in general. There's a lot of good music out there, but music is not my forte. I am confused enough. I don't need to listen to anyone else's lyrics. I have more than enough music running through my own head half the time. But yeah, it happened with the beatniks in the 60s-

GG: That whole bullshit coffeeshop thing. All that *crap.*

15

SF: The hippies, too. And in the 20s, with Gertrude Stein. The whole F. Scott Fitzgerald thing. These are *ideas*, and they were people who were equally fucking depressed, washed out, ex-patriots for some reas-*oh, I wonder why*. But who lumped each other together, licked each other's wounds, and thus became strong! By the way, how do you keep a hippie from drowning?

GG: I don't know.

SF: Take your foot off his head.

GG: Hahahaha!

SF: It starts out political, and then it becomes fashion. The big boys with the padded wallets will eventually decide, "okay, we can make money off this." So then, people don't *have* to leave their computer. They don't *have to* get off the fuckin couch. They just have to go to the fuckin mall. Stasis. That's why I prefer *no* stardom.

GG: You can "be" whatever you want as a celebrity. As a real person, you can only be yourself. You have to actually live what you say you are.

SF: I am trying to be somewhat inclusive. I don't want somebody to ever look at a comic I've done, or some drunken babble I've written or posted somewhere, and say "I can't do that." I am not a musician, but every rock show I've ever seen, with a few exceptions, I've always thought, "I could get up there and do that."

GG: Odds are, when you go to a rock show, you're going to see something really boring.

SF: What it all comes down to is everyone *can* do it themselves, if they at least try. It's about being true to yourself. Who else do you really have to worry about? In that respect, it's good to be selfish. But by being true to yourself, you are also helping other people out. To me, that's equally important.

GG: That's an infectious idea.

SF: Contaminate! I am here to contaminate. This is contamination *station*, baby.

GG: Let's hang out later.

SF: Well, I think I have someone else pencilled in on the dancecard. It's a medicinal release. The buildup and release, hormonal balance. I wouldn't want to-

GG: Okay. You're horny. So I shouldn't feel insulted.

SF: It's time for me to do some community service.

GG: So you think you're some kind of stud?
SF: Well, you'd kinda have to be there. And today, I'm not giving out free samples.


    Frida drives me back to my motel when I begin to slur my words. I hang out in the motel bar and watch that television show Buffy the Vampire Slayer for the first time. (It's actually quite good, give it a chance if you haven't yet.) Then I walk back across the bridge into the city to pick up cash at the Western Union office, located within the Portland Greyhound station. The Sex & Guts gang have all chipped in to save my ass. Kurt Lee sends me one hundred dollars, and demands that I drink every penny. Kurt Lee is a genius.

    I have a drink in a classy hotel, where I am given dirty looks. The drink costs $6. I shouldn't have come here, I'm thinking. I sit down next to a pretty girl outside the Hotel and talk to her about botany. Can I kiss you I ask. No, and don't ask me again. Can I touch your hair I ask. No, and I'm not changing my mind. How about a handshake then. She laughs and says okay. I wish her and her plants a long and happy life.

    I'm trudging sockless in boots, because of my toe, and because wearing only one sock creates balance problems. (I'm very delicate.)


    It's dark again.


    Walking across the bridge, I undo my belt and descend some stairs at the midway point. I have it out, my lonely fucking balls aching with bladder pressure.
I say aloud, drunk again, "I will not piss on this town. That would be bad karma."
  I have never been moved to extend such a gesture to a city.
  I have never been so in love with anywhere.
  My mouth tastes like ten ashtrays.

# FEBRUARY 4, 2003

GERALDINE, black whore

G: Whatchoo doin in there with the door hangin wide open?

GG: Talking.

G: Yeah, I was hearin. You sayin some freaky shit. Whatchoo talkin about?

GG: Jack the Ripper.

G: You freaky dude.

GG: I know. I'm insane.

G: That thing on?

GG: Yes.

G: Turn that shit off. I don't want my voice on no muhfuckin tape.

GG: Okay.

G: Guy at the bar says you work for Rolling Stone.

GG: Yeah.

G: But you broke.

GG: They don't pay me. Jan Wenner says-

G: Who?

GG: My editor.

G: He don't pay you?

GG: He says I'll just spend it on beer.

G: Gimme a beer.

GG: Gimme a blowjob.

G: Gimme that beer. And quit actin like a fuckin retard, I'll beat the fuck outta yoo.

GG: Help yourself.

G: I'll be back up to see you later.

GG: No you won't.

# FEBRUARY 3, 2003

APPX: 6 P.M.

I head to Dante's to do some interviews and see Satanica. I find her boyfriend and try to flatter him by saying I initially didn't want to show up because I was afraid he'd trounce me. He has no idea who I am, and I am later told that he was freaked out by the encounter.

Dante's basement
Fist City, rock'n'roll band

GG: You motherfuckers rock.
FCG: Thank you.
GG: Where did the name come from?
FCG: In comes from-
GG: Because *Fist City* is a mean, nasty, graphic, disturbing name.
FCG: It comes from the Loretta Lynne song. She also has an album with the same title.

TAPE MANGLES

GG: Based on the amount of tape that was destroyed, I think I only lost thirty seconds, but would you mind singing it again?
FIST CITY: (hand claps with female and male vocals) "No grave, hold this body down there ain't no grave / coldest part of town / hear that trumpet sound / gotta get up out the ground they ain't no grave / hold this body down there ain't no train / getting all the hooch I need there ain't no train / carry all the hooch I need / hear that cuckoo sound / gotta get up outta the ground there ain't no train / carry all the hooch I need there ain't no grave / hold this body down there ain't no grave / hold this body down / hear that trumpet sound / gotta get up out of the ground there ain't no grave / hold this body down / looked up over Jordan and what did I see? / so many angels starin back at me / there ain't no grave / hold this body down there ain't no grave / hold this body down / when you hear that trumpet sound /

19

gotta get up outta the ground there ain't no grave / hold this body down / there ain't no pussy-"

GG: There's no pussy?

FC: "Get this whiskey off my mind there ain't enough pussy / cheap whiskey on my mind, when I lift it to my lips / but no relief do I find there ain't no pussy / hold this body down there ain't no grave / hold this body down there ain't no grave. Hold this body down."

TAPE CUTS

GG: What inspires the obsession with darkness in your songs?

FIST CITY GUITARIST: I don't know, maybe-

GG: Portland?

FCG: No, I would say it's more to do with relationships that haven't gone so good.

FIST CITY SINGER: Love lost. Love forfeited.

GG: You guys can't break up. You're too good. You're really fuckin good! I loved your set. I lived in New York City for four years and spent two years in LA, but I'm a country bumpkin, you know. That's why I got run out of them both, because I am a country bumpkin and I can't function in the big city.

FCG: I'm a country bumpkin too.

GG: I'm talking about myself too much. My point is, I never saw much live music in either place that I really liked. But you guys were *fucking incredible*!

FCS: Thank you!

FCG: I felt good tonight.

GG: Thank you for the interview.

FCG: Thank you, man.

Jenny, audience member

GG: What do you do here?

JENNY: I'm just here for the anniversary party.

GG: So what do you do?

J: I work at Cost Plus Imports.

GG: What do you do to amuse yourself when you're not working?

J: Pretty much something like this.

GG: What's the best thing about Portland?

J: The diversity. The people are great. When you're in other places, they don't have as much pride as people in Portland have. People around here are really proud of where they're from and who they are.

GG: They're very generous, too. It's very easy to talk to people here.

J: Yeah. Portland is friendly and easygoing and laid back. It's a good place to be.

TAPE CUTS

Cole Baker, audience member

GG: What do you do in Portland?

CB: Sometimes I come around here and play Pool.

GG: What do you like most about Portland?

CB: People are really nice here. You don't have to worry about getting shot at just walking down the street. Diversity. It's safe.

GG: I have here eight dollars left to my name. What I need is cigarettes and beer. In my position, what would you do?

CB: I would just take things as they go. I never worry.

GG: Is that the Portland way?

CB: I would say so.

GG: In Portland, it seems to be possible to have faith in things. Travel in God's channel.

CB: I am not a man of faith.

GG: Me neither really.

CB: I just take it as it goes. I place no faith in any external sources, only in myself.

GG: It's a very lucky town. Lots of good things can happen, all you have to do is stay in one place long enough. I'm having a ball.

CB: I think there's a lot of heart here. There's a lot of people who can relate to each other. The economy is shitty right now and there's a lot of people who are understanding because they're in the same situation themselves. There's a lot of empathy. A lot of heart.

GG: What are my chances of bumming two bucks out there in the street?

CB: It's not uncommon.

GG: I may not look poor but that doesn't matter. I may not look broke. But you don't have to here. People can tell.

CB: If you level with people here, they understand. I don't know how to explain that, but…it doesn't matter if you're white or you're black. It's more of a class thing. Some people might get the wrong idea, some people might not. It's an attitude. Regardless of where you're coming from, it's…

GG: It's the look in your eyes.

CB: Exactly. Yeah!

TAPE CUTS

MATTHEW, audience member
Curtis, drunken monkey

GG: What do you do, sir?

M: I am the assistant director of religious education at a First Unitarian Church.

GG: Would you agree that while Hollywood may be beautiful, it is in many ways like so much rotting garbage?

M: Garbage is a *nice* word for it.

GG: Yeah, it is more forgiving than "shit".

M: Refuse. Mastication of purification.

GG: Do you think that Portland is one of the best cities going in this country today?

M: Definitely. I had a lot of cities to choose from and I picked Portland.

GG: Why?

CURTIS: Get out of the way, I got business in here. Do you always interview people in Portland bathrooms?

GG: (laughing)

C: Looking for a fight?

GG: (laughing) Hey look at her. I think she can see your dick.

C: *Hey good lookin*! *Who ya been kissin*? I'm pissin *blood* because I done just busted a nut on that bitch!

GG: That's harsh, man.

C: Sorry, dude. I could have just written it on the bathroom wall, but I thought I'd just talk to you.
GG: That's nice of you. I know I am pretentious and obnoxious, but I'm just doing my job.

TAPE CUTS

Amy, artist

GG: I get the feeling of there being a real sense of justice in Portland.
A: I don't know, I think that it's a dirtier city than most. I think that there's this fantasy of Portland, much like San Francisco, of it being this gentle city of peace and love, and fairy tale bullshit, which isn't true. This is one of the dirtiest cities that I've been to, far worse than New York in many respects. In this city I get my tit grabbed, but in New York it never happened to me in my life.
GG: Maybe it's a good town for a man, but not for a woman.
A: Okay. So where is Jim Goad?

Jim Goad, author

GG: I talked shit about you in a public forum, why would you even consider letting me interview you?
JG: Well, you're a fuckup, but I think you've got a good heart.
GG: Why did you move to Portland?
JG: Every bad thing that has ever happened to me, happened here. I mean, aside from getting slapped around as a kid, *every bad thing* happened to me here. Debbie died, beating up Sky, going to jail.

I exit the club, and turn towards the bridge. Jim calls out behind me. He says "take care of that foot." I'm deliberately missing Satanica's performance.

Back at the motel, I drink what's left of the beer and make faces at myself in the mirror. I find ten dollars in my briefcase and spend it on five vodkas. The bar is empty all night, so I slur observations about things I think I might forget, taping over 90% of my interview with Jim Goad. A woman knocks on my door a few hours later,

23

looking for matches. I tell her I'm looking for drugs. How much ya got? Nothing. How ya gonna pay for it? I can do things, I tell her. I'll be back, she says. I watch out the window to see her disappear into a room across the parking lot. I wait an hour, shakes coming on again, before going to that room across the parking lot, pound on the door. It opens by itself on the third blow. In the room are three women, none of them are the one who needed matches. The table is a filthy explosion of dirty needles, blackened spoons, and cigarette butts. One of the woman has a needle in her arm. I ask for a shot. You over there in 229? Yeah. I'll bring you something later. No you won't, I say.

In my room, I find a beer under the bed, finish half before passing out in a pile of condom wrappers and cassette tapes.

# FEBRUARY 2, 2003

APPX. 6 P.M.

MISS SATANICA
Portland Bar Crawl Tape One

BAR NUMBER ONE
MS: I'm roping in all the hot chicks.
GG: I'm roping in *everything*.

TAPE CUTS

MS: Ma'am? We're doing a story on Portland together. And you're the hottest punk rock barmaid in all of Portland. I say you're too young, but you're still pretty good. Have a seat, we're going to interview you!
HOTTEST PUNK ROCK BARMAID IN PORTLAND: What's this for?
MS: Sex & Guts Magazine Online!
GG: (staring directly at barmaid) What is it about Portland that makes me feel like I've already died and gone to Heaven, do you think?
BARMAID: There are a lot of good looking people here.
GG: It's the *perfect* town.
BARMAID: There's a shitload of drunks.
GG: How long have you worked in this bar?
BARMAID: About a year and a half.
GG: Where are you from?
BARMAID: Seattle.
GG: How long have you been here?
BARMAID: Five years.
GG: Do you ever imagine leaving here?
BARMAID: Yes.
GG: Why, for God's sake?
BARMAID: Because as far as I'm concerned, this place is endearing, but it's an overgrown logging town.
MS: Where do you want to go?

BARMAID: I would like to just up and move somewhere I've never been before, like Prague. Even if I could only go for four days.

TAPE CUTS

MS: Gene, you're going to have to hold the microphone steady.
GG: Okay.
MS: I want to go down on that barmaid.
GG: Just ask her and you can do it in the bathroom. I'll sneak in and tape record it.
MS: She looks like a girl that could handle it on tape. Goddamn, *why aren't we on Girls Gone Wild?* Why AREN'T we?
GG: Why don't you ask her that question?
MS: For the record, I always wanted to meet the person in charge of *Girls Gone Wild*, because it's just stupid men so far, who are doing it, and I could get such better footage. Instead of all these lecherous old men saying "show us your tits", let Miss Satanica do it! I will tell you one thing: *all girls LOVE* me. Even if they're not into girls, they'll say "well, I'm not really into girls, but I'm kind of into you." That's my fucking CURSE!
GG: But she doesn't seem to be willing.
MS: Which sucks, because with other girls we could do it.
GG: Is she or is she not going to let you go down on her?
MS: Probably, because I get more first timers than anybody else on the planet.
GG: Let's have another drink, wait and see what happens.
MS: No, we're only here for *one*. And she's here until 1 A.M. We're only covering three blocks, baby.

TAPE CUTS

GG: I think I just sang every word on that entire record. *L.A.M.F.* I think Miss Satanica's ears are bleeding now.

TAPE CUTS:

GG: What the fuck just happened back there?
MS: We just got thrown out of a bar for *absolutely no reason.*

26

GG: Which is an amazing thing, really.

MS: If there are two drunken monkies in the world who can do that, it's you and me.

GG: We did it! Yaaay!

MS: We got thrown out for no fuckin reason.

GG: Well, I did eat three olives out of the cocktail tray.

MS: And I ate three olives and a few slices of oranges, but...*I was willing to pay for it*!

GG: I'm willing to pay for it still! They didn't even give us a fucking chance. They threw us out.

MS: Unceremoniously! We were thrown out unceremoniously. So I had to create the ceremony.

GG: Well, I did put a match out on your tongue.

MS: The public was on our side!

GG: They loved it! What was your ceremony, dear Satanica?

MS: What?

GG: After the guy told us he wouldn't serve us any drinks. I said, "you're a fuckin snob!"

TAPE CUTS

MS: I say fuck all of you! Let's suck our oysters.

GG: These look good.

MS: Then we'll hit the next bar.

GG: They're too hot to eat.

MS: These look *gooood* though.

GG: Leave those alone and let them cool off. You'll burn your mouth. So what happened?

MS: We were thrown out for *noooo reason*!

GG: We've already established that. So what happened next?

MS: I flashed my tits. (giggling)

GG: And then?

MS: The public was on our side. My tits have that effect on people. The public loves my tits.

GG: So do I. But they *applauded*!

MS: I can smell you over the oysters.

GG: That's my natural scent.

27

TAPE CUTS

MS: *We're in drunken monkey town*! We're two drunk monkies in the drunken monkey town! This is a town for *drunken monkeys*! We're *in our element*!
GG: We finally found our way home!
MS: We're in our element! Let's ride it! All the way to the end!
GG: We're going to!
MS: *I know*! I've shown you every bar, have I not?
GG: Yes, dear.
MS: I'm good like that!

TAPE CUTS

MS: I'm starting to catch a buzz.
GG: I'm definitely catching a buzz. But we've had like ten drinks each!
MS: Six bars!
GG: And we're drinking *beer on top of those*!
MS: A lot of these drinks were free!
GG: We're getting a lot of free shit tonight!
MS: YEAH!
GG: How many times have I flashed my dick so far?
MS: Only two.
GG: Oh, and you know, I'm not even behaving this way because I'm drunk. I'm just really *happy*!

TAPE CUTS

MS: I am a *terrifle influence* on you Gene!
GG: *Terrifle*?
MS: I am a TERRIFLE INFLUENCE ON YOU GENE, hah hah hah!

TAPE CUTS

MS: That was all it was ever really meant to be.

GG: We are now blazing a hellish path through downtown Portland. There will be no stopping us now. I mean, really? What's going to happen? Is the world going to explode? Before this is all over?
MS: No, just your cock. That's off the record, you *BASTARD*!
GG: HAHAHAHA! Too late!
MS: Look at the sky! I said, LOOK AT THIS FUCKING-

We visit two buildings where Miss Satanica used to live. On the roof of the second place, I leave her to her thoughts and ignore my fear of heights long enough to appreciate the awe inspiring beauty of bird's-eye-view Portland. We stumble back down the fire escape and find ourselves locked in the basement. "This is where the alcoholics live," she tells me. I imagine Satanica cooking breakfast for the alcoholics, and feeding them, one by one. We begin pounding on the door leading to their dimly lit basement hallway. "LET US IN! LET US IN!" I tell her to calm down, seeing another door behind the fire escape. It opens out to the street. We escape, running to the next bar, laughing.

TAPE CUTS

Christina, record story clerk

GG: What makes Portland so cool?
Christina: People are genuine.
GG: What do you think makes people so genuine here, as opposed to other places?
C: Desire.
GG: Oh, *WOW*! Your name?
C: Christina.

TAPE CUTS

John Callahan, cartoonist

GG: How would you describe your cartoon artwork?
JC: My cartoons? I guess they're just totally disagreeable to people. They're completely off-the-wall, but to me they seem normal. I must

be personally very warped, because they seem so normal to me. Other people get very riled up and upset. They have shit hemmorhages.

GG: Shit hemmorhages?

JC: (laughs) Whatever the word is.

GG: What kind of content is it that would upset people?

JC: Unpleasant life experiences such as divorce or amputation. Death. I was published in the London Observer for many years, and one of my cartoons was Laurel and Hardy together in bed in the AIDS ward.

GG: (laughing)

JC: They're dying. And Hardy is saying to Laurel, "here's another fine mess you've gotten us into."

GG: (laughing)

MS: The reason we came in here, is because of the universe.

GG: We are being taken care of by some unseen force tonight. Miss Satanica had been looking for you, and now she's found you, because she had a feeling about this store. And here you are. Thing is, we're traveling in God's channel.

MS: We came in here for a *reason* tonight!

JC: Yeah! Oh another thing about my cartoons is that Dr. Laura always reads them over her radio show. One cartoon was Jesus Christ on a cross, and he's hanging on the cross, tired and weary. And he's thinking to himself, "T.G.I.F." I was just on Comedy Central with Dave Attel and-is that thing working?

GG: Yeah. Satanica said that you know Tom Waits.

JC: He's a friend of mine, he likes my cartoons. And he liked one of my songs.

GG: You write songs too?

JC: Yeah. There's a guy in LA who sings some of my songs in a bar. I'm trying to get famous people to sing my songs.

GG: You're in a wheelchair. What happened?

JC: I was paralyzed in a car wreck in LA. I should mention the name of my book. It's called "Don't Worry, He Won't Get Far on Foot".

GG: Ha ha ha!

JC: On the cover is a broken down wheelchair, this empty, abandoned, broken down wheelchair in the desert. It shows these posse guys on horses. They've been tracking this wheelchair.

GG: (laughing)

JC: That's my signature cartoon, I guess. I get to meet a lot of interesting people. I was on 60 Minutes. I sold my life story to Robin Williams for a movie.

MS: I forgot. Robin Williams wants to play you.

JC: Yeah, he bought the rights to my life story.

GG: You know Robin Williams?

JC: I go down there to San Francisco and stay with him.

MS: Didn't he want you to sober up, and then he offered to buy the rights?

JC: Yeah.

MS: You were a *crazy* drunkard for a long time.

JC: I was about 22 years old, in LA. I lived in LA. I was the passenger in a car which was being driven by a drunk person. I was paralyzed. Rehabilitated in Downey, which was weird. But I liked Downey because the famous guitar player from the Blasters, Dave Alvin, is there.

GG: I love the Blasters.

MS: I love them too.

JC: I got to meet him at a Patti Smith concert a few years ago. He likes my cartoons. I'm trying to get him to sing one of my songs.

MS: John's the fucking bomb.

GG: I know I've seen your work before! But I can't-

MS: That's because you're from the east coast, darlin.

GG: Did you ever work for National Lampoon?

JC: Yes I did, actually.

GG: Okay, *that's how I know your work*! They were great, really great! Now I remember them! You did one about a whorehouse and the joke was something about a girl on her period.

JC: Yeah.

GG: See?

MS: John's bad *ass*.

STORE CLERK: Could you try to be a little quieter?

GG: Let's get out of here.

MS: Yeah.


APPX. 10 PM

TAPE CUTS

MS: I like that house back there.
GG: Let's run back and pound on their door.

TAPE CUTS


BETHANY, homeowner

B: Yes? Who are you?
GG: We just felt strangely compelled by your house and we wanted
to come and say hello.
B: Hello.
GG:: I'm doing a story on Portland for Rolling Stone magazine.
Why do you love living here?
B: Because we always like to eat out at night and there's so many
great restaurants.
MS: My hair is fantastic, is it not? I was looking for a cru-da-tat, do
you have that here?
B: Uh…
MS: A coup'detat!
B: No, I don't have that.
GG: Is that a drink? What are you talking about? She's drunk. Well
thank you for your time! It was very lovely meeting you.
B: Thank you.
GG: What are your dogs' names?
B: Jerry and Lyle.
GG: And your name?
B: Bethany.
MS: We have work to do now.
GG: Bye!

TAPE CUTS

(street)
GG: Are you serious? That was the last bar?
MS: No more.
GG: No more?

MS: No more. But I'm still coming home with you, doesn't that make it better?

GG: Yeah, but…

MS: Don't be sad.

GG: I was hoping that this night would last forever, at least for a few more hours. This has been the greatest night of my entire life. You're the most fun girl I've ever met. And if it weren't for-

MS: Don't cry. I hate that shit.

GG: So do I. I wasn't gonna. But still-

MS: Hold on a second, I'm running back to that bar.

GG: Why? SATANICA!

MS: DON'T GO ANYWHERE!

GG: OKAY, I'LL WAIT!


TAPE CUTS


GG: What the hell's that for?

MS: To light our way home.

GG: You stole their candle?

MS: Ha ha ha.

GG: Cup your hands over it. It's gonna go out.

MS: I know where we can get a bus.


TAPE CUTS


MS: Mmmm Kali, la meee naa. Mmmm Kali la meee naa.

GG: You *are* Kali, aren't you? You must be my angel of death.

MS: Angel of *life*.

GG: And of death. What did you say before, about our journey?

MS: This is the end of our journey.

GG: You stole a candle. It's been such an amazing night, that I'm thinking about…well, we're in Heaven, aren't we?

MS: YEAH!

GG: But we're going to Hell. We might be in Heaven again, then back to Hell. Around like that, for a few more years. Then we're going to die. When it's all over, do we go to the *real* Heaven?

MS: We're in that realm, as we speak.

GG: What about when it's over?

MS: It's never over.

GG: We'll leave the candle here to mark our passing.

MS: I'm leaving it.

GG: You're leaving the candle.

MS: Yeah.

GG: Because the night is over.

MS: Yeah.

GG: I guess this was our night for Portland. You'll be with *him* tomorrow.

MS: I'm sorry, baby. Don't be mad.

GG: Well, it'll just burn here until it goes out. And whoever comes by, until it goes out, will think something important happened here. They won't know you, and they won't know me. But they'll *know* something *really* important happened here.

MS: (laughs quietly) Yeah..

GG: This is where it ends.

[kissing]

MS: You are the only thing that doesn't irritate my tongue. (laughing)

GG: Well, what do you expect after you put a dozen flaming torches out in your fucking mouth? There's gonna be repercussions, baby.

MS: (laughs)

GG: This was our night for Portland. We're leaving the candle to mark our passing. To mark the end of *our* night. That's romantic, isn't it?

MS: Yeah, is is. Oh baby, I'm so sorry.

GG: Don't matter. Let's go home. Say goodnight.

MS: Goodnight, Gracie.

# FEBRUARY 1, 2003

APPX. 12:30 AM
MISS SATANICA
Fire Dancer

GG: Why fire?
MS: Redemption.
GG: How did you get so good at it?
MS: It was innate.
GG: Do you always answer your questions so tersely?
MS: Sometimes. (laughs)
GG: You're fucking with me.
MS: Because you're sticking something in my face!
GG: What would you rather I used? If they would invent some kind of technology which did not require me to be a chauvinistic pig I would use it. But until then-
MS: Ask more pertinent questions, and I will answer with more than one word.
GG: I'm a lousy interviewer. My pretty microphone is going to hell.

TAPE CUTS

GG: I always like to involve myself personally with my interview subjects.
MS: Haven't you already?
GG: Yeah, we just a great fuck.
MS: Is this on the record?
GG: I'll decide that later.
MS: I plead the fifth. Unless I am guaranteed a really good catfight for money. (laughs)
GG: That is directed to Lydia.
MS: Only for money! Just for fun and profit. I want to be friends. And for the record, calling me dangerously insane was like saying Martha Stewart is a good housekeeper.
GG: Whoah.
MS: (laughs) I feel like I have a vote of confidence. I am on the right track, obviously.

GG: You have great tits, by the way.

MS: (laughs)

GG: We've had a few drunken nights together, like the time the cops nearly shot me.

MS: That's nothing. I've had so many guns pointed at my head. Do you want to hear my favorite "gun pointed at my head" story?

GG: If I publish this, Lydia will never have any sympathy for me again, ever.

MS: Well, maybe you shouldn't publish this. Some people should have private art in their own private collections, that they only whip out for certain beatiful equations. Something private.

GG: I think that *everything* has to come out now.

MS: No. When I work at orgies, for the rich and famous, that's for my personal collection. I am not a person that likes to lay my life out in the open, for people to dissect.

GG: You have final approval on the content of this article.

MS: Do you want to hear my favorite "gun pointed at the head" story?

GG: Yesh.

MS: I'd just got done working on *Casper 3* as a scenic. It was my very first paycheck, from the guys that do *Mighty Morphin Power Rangers*.

GG: You're beautiful.

MS: Would you *shut up*? This is my story. I was working for Sabaan, with Cathy Moriarty and-

GG: The actress?

MS: Yeah.

GG: She's so great.

MS: And Teri Garr! There was another actress, I can't remember. Bernice bobs her hair.

GG: Bernice Bobs O'Hare?

MS: She played Olive Oil.

GG: That would be Shelley Duvall, dear.

MS: So we go to the wrap party, and I get there with my drunkest boyfriend *ever*. He makes you look like a little baby.

GG: Quite the contrary. I am King Baby. I have no talent for drinking whatsoever.

MS: He is such a drunk that he makes you look like an infant. Baby, you have so many more years ahead of you, drinkin.

GG: Don't tell me these things.

MS: You're an amateur…so…

GG: But I am a damn fine interviewer, and I can interview damn fine while drunk, so leave me alone.

MS: So, for the record, you are an amateur.

GG: My hands shake just as bad as anyone's in the morning, I guarantee you. But since I don't know how to act sober, I always run the risk of being even worse if I decide to get drunk.

MS: You're good as an interview but as a drunk, you have many years ahead of you.

GG: FUCK!

MS: People can tell that I drink too much. I always get extra drink tickets no matter where I go. I don't even have to say anything, they just hand them to me. They just pulled the roll, and gave us drink tickets when they saw us coming.

GG: Can I put my hand under your shirt while I talk to you?

MS: Sure. You've gotta squeeze the nipples though.

GG: Oh.

MS: We drink all night and then decide to go back to downtown LA where the loft is. Fourth and Alameda is a rough part of town. We decided we wanted to do the *bad sex in the alley*-thing. In the dirty crack alley, for thrills. We're thrill seekers. I'm in my truck, a Ford F1250. (laughs)

GG: You have beautiful eyes.

MS: Thank you. So do you.

GG: Thank you.

MS: (laughing) Your eyes are almost as beautiful as your cock, Gene.

GG: Uh…

MS: So anyway, we're in the back of my Ford F1250, and of course I am wearing a crotchless body suit with this hot dress. We decide to start fucking doggie-style and I've got my head out the window of the truck.

GG: (groaning)

MS: This is long before you. This is in the past. I am getting totally pounded, perfectly. Having a great time. BAM BAM BAM BAM.

My head hanging out thinking,, "wow, this is fuckin great." All of a
sudden this car pulls up. This little Toyota piece of shit. A guy
jumps out going, "CAN I WATCH? CAN I WATCH?"

GG: "Sure buddy, how much ya got?"

MS: Exactly. I said, "okay".

GG: You let him watch for free?

MS: Yeah. And all of a sudden I hear, "LAPD!" I have this big ass
dick in my fuckin pussy, and a gun in my face, and it was...*HOT*.

GG: You sick fuckin BITCH!

MS: But-

GG: No.

MS: I-

GG: You're out of your fucking mind.

MS: But I didn't *know* that I would feel that way, okay? I was
confronted with something and I made a decision, where it
became...HOT!

GG: I feel sorry for-

MS: I had no choice. I was peaking out at an orgasm, with a gun in
my face. Therefore I was conditioned. It's like a fuckin *rat*, in a
fuckin cage, with a piece of fuckin cheese, and a fuckin electrode,
okay? I didn't have a choice, I was turned on. The cop was kinda
hot. And all I could say was, "I'M NOT A WHORE!" And my
boyfriend was like, "SHE'S NOT A WHORE!"

GG: (laughing) Your boyfriend was mistaken.

MS: The cop realized, a minute later. He says, "call off backup. It's
just a couple *thrill seekers*." That is the gun at my head story.

GG: Great story.

MS: Well...the cock helped. The gun wouldn't have been so good
without the cock, okay?

GG: Yeah, yeah, yeah.

MS: Is that the end of my interview?

GG: Fuck no! How about this: where were you at the age of 19?

MS: I had just seen *Suburbia*, right? The next thing I know, it has
manifested. I was living in a burnt out, Victorian squat. It was called
"Hellsquat". In Philadelphia, with Paradox and Jack Rabbit. They
were really nice guys. I was still a virgin. These crazy people were
all really nice to me.

GG: How old were you when you lost your virginity?

38

MS: I was 20. Well, no it happened earlier, but that was date rape. The guy horsefucked me until I had to go to the hospital, on a waterbed. I have had an adversity to waterbeds since that moment when I was 17. But I was asking for it, because I wasn't wearing a bra that night. (laughing)

GG: I'm sorry about all that. But all you can do is laugh.

MS: I'm good at that.

GG: You have to be good at that.

MS: But I can look back on it now, and go-

GG: I'm being melodramatic.

MS: Yeah, a little. I went to a party, I got drunk. I love Camille Paglia, because she's right in so many ways. You shouldn't put yourself in a position like that if you can't depend on yourself. You can't depend on a man, to be the bigger fucking person, ever.

GG: Nor can you count on a white man especially, because what I said to Bobby was-

MS: Which brings me to when I lost my virginity for *real*. (laughs) This drunk ass redneck…he was a fuckin farmboy wearing one of those fuckin shirts, with the fuckin mother of pearl buttons, fucking me. All of a sudden I had blood clots coming out of me the size of softballs. I had to go to the hospital. I'd been thrown out of the mental institutions. The girls homes. The foster homes. *And* my parents' house. My mom, dad, and brother all held me down and beat me until I was bloody, and then I went back to Idaho. Then I got raped. I think that hospital bill is still pending. I went back to Philadelphia and fell in love. My first love was this beautiful black man. He taught me how to *fuck*. I know how to *fuck* now because of him! For the record, I was biting my hand.

GG: But you're with me tonight, so let's the skip the black dude and move on to the fire dancing.

MS: You're measuring up so far, Gene.

GG: What about the toe story? I like that one.

MS: You mean ten minutes ago? Well, I had a cigarette between my toes and I gave you a drag and you tried to suck really hard on it to burn my toes. Then what happened?

GG: I almost died. Well, that's an exaggeration. But it made me sick.

MS: Alright then. So what happens when you fuck with Satanica?

GG: You wind up in a very bad place.
MS: Ask Jim Goad.
GG: I love Jim Goad. Dearly.
MS: Opinions are like assholes.
GG: I like yours.
MS: And it likes you.

TAPE CUTS

GG: I want to do that again, but on tape this time.
MS: You dirty bird. No.
GG: But I want to.
MS: You're so sincere.
GG: I'll cry.
MS: Okay, turn off the tape.

TAPE CUTS

MS: <slurp> <slurp> <slurp> Whatcha thinkin Gene?
GG: Uh…I love you?
MS: (laughs) Men are so easy.
GG: You're going to marry me, right?
MS: Nnnnn-no.

TAPE CUTS

MS: Can't you come without jerking off?
GG: No. Not unless I can fuck you without a condom.
MS: For the record, Satanica uses condoms.
GG: For the record, Gene *don't*.
MS: For the record, did he just use one?
GG: For the record, yeah, but only for you.
MS: I bet you say that to all the girls.

TAPE CUTS

GG: Your performance goes beyond the whole idea of watching a
naked or half naked woman onstage. Because you're using *fire*,

threatening to damage not only your mouth, but your tits and your cunt, too. You are threatening the audience with the destruction of everything that makes you physically beautiful as a woman.

MS: That's because if you want to fuckin objectify me, I'll shove it up your ass.

GG: That's your philosophy?

MS: No, it's more about the idea of turning the objectification around.

GG: I get that, but it still upsets me.

MS: Sometimes it takes big measures. I have had guys get really confused by what I do. Or some of them say they have to think, that it gives them a lot to think about. It's beautiful and it's dangerous, but it is the juxtaposition of objectification.

GG: Would you consider yourself an alcoholic?

MS: Well, sure. And it's probably gonna fuckin kill me and it's gonna make me ugly. It will destroy me, but…I'll sleep when I'm dead. I don't know. I tried to kill myself with drinking, and that takes a lot of hard work and dedication.

GG: That's a hard way to go down.

MS: It just takes too much dedication. It's like killing the [DELETED], I just don't have enough energy for that. But I have a plan, though. I figure that there must be some people out there with a lot of energy, so I wanted to take up a collection where everyone throws in ten dollars for the hitman who will kill the [DELETED]. Therefore, you can be apathetic, yet everyone's doing something. It's like Bruce Springsteen, pulling people together. Ten dollars is *not* a lot of money, and somebody could do it. I don't even want anyone to kill him, I just want someone to yank him out by his fuckin Alfred E. Neuman ears, and I want to see him get his fuckin *ass kicked*. That would be so great to see him get his fuckin face pounded in. I know how *I'd* kick the shit out of him. I have a whole plan. I'd kick the fuck out of him. First I'd grab him by his big ass ears, and then I'd just yank his ear over my goddamn knee as hard as I fuckin could. That's my favorite move.

GG: This is my first ever nude interview.

MS: Nuh *uh*!

GG: Yeah it is.

41

MS: What about all those other girls you write into your fuckin magazine, *Gene*?

GG: What girls?

MS: The A-girls. The A-list.

GG: Amy and Annie?

MS: What's with this thing about you throwing yourself headlong into love? Don't you know *love is for suckers*?

GG: You have opened my eyes. I give up.

MS: You can't just fall in love with every girl that can write a fuckin poem, because there's *so* many poems out there, and so many girls. You've got a lot of cock, but I don't think it's enough to go around. (laughing)

GG: Well…in any case, why don't we go to sleep now?

MS: Well, why don't you tell me? Can I interview you?

GG: Yeah, if you want to.

MS: So, this might be painful, but-

GG: Can I have a cigarette?

MS: Yes. I want to know what happened with Annie?

GG: Annie?

MS: Annie. She doesn't even write in to the website anymore, what did you do to her?

GG: I didn't do anything to her.

MS: What happened?

GG: I don't wanna talk about it.

MS: How old is she?

GG: 31. I'm trying to just get a little work done. I don't get paid for it. I do it because I feel like I have to.

MS: That *is* the plight of the artist.

GG: I know that.

MS: But you were in love. So let's talk about why you fall in love easily.

GG: I didn't love her.

MS: You told me you were.

GG: I was in a state of alcoholic dementia at the time.

MS: Do you think you fall in love with women for what they write?

GG: No.

MS: Than what was it?

GG: I don't know.

MS: That she loved you.

GG: Yeah.

MS: Where is she now?

GG: I don't want to talk about her.

MS: Have you spoken to her since?

GG: Yeah, I did. But I can say about Amy, because I have already been with her, and I do love her. I miss her. And I can say that I wish things hadn't gone down the way they did. The fact of the matter is that I *do* find her attractive, and I do respect her writing.. Look, I came here to Portland to fuckin see her. It didn't go right. But what happened? I saw you perform for the very first time, which was worth the trip in itself. It was amazing.

MS: I rock.

GG: Yeah, you do rock. But it was amazing.

MS: I work hard for it. Just like you work hard for your writing. People work hard in all different ways.

GG: And I got to talk to Bobby.

MS: Maybe you learned a life lesson about trying to break and destroy what you love. Amy will be a nice lesson for you. Maybe you won't fuck up the next girl. If you really loved her. Hopefully you really loved her enough to know that you fucked her up so you won't fuck up anyone else.

GG: I think she's too tough for this to have fucked her up. All I did was make her sick and disgusted.

MS: How old is she?

GG: 27.

MS: Oh, she's in her Saturn return. She can't be dating you. Saturn returns are the worst, nobody should *ever* date then. I've been in California way too long and I talk about the fucking planets but there's something to be said for them. And you're going to hit yours. In your Saturn return Gene, it's either going to make you a man or it's gonna fucking kill you. You better make your fucking choice now.

GG: I believe I have. I'm alive, aren't I?

MS: No, it's going to hit you in a year.

GG: If it gets worse than this man, then the fucking wolves can have me, I don't give a shit. It ain't worth it.

43

MS: Don't be a pussy. You're talking like that to a *woman*. You *pussy*. It gets a lot harder.

GG: Yeah, so what. If I get too tired, I am going to sleep. Simple as that. Let it get harder. I will *gladly* commit suicide. I don't want this, and I'm not going to tolerate it. I don't need this fuckin shit.

MS: Then you're just going to come back as a beetle that eats cow dung. You'll have to start over again anyway. Do you really want that?

GG: I don't give one good fuck for even the very concept of the afterlife. It does not concern me whatsoever.

MS: You better fucking face it.

GG: No I'm *not* going to face it. Why should I have to?

MS: Face it later, your choice. (laughs)

GG: I don't believe in it.

MS: Then why don't you go to India?

GG: Why not just get my toenails pulled out by a Vietnemese scumbag, and stay home?

MS: India is really nice. It's a lot better than what you just suggested.

GG: I would prefer to avoid it.

MS: It was the most beautiful thing I have ever seen, to see bodies burnt in a pile 24/7 right in front of me.

GG: Because you're a sick fucking cunt, that's why.

MS: That's a curse, really. (laughs) It's beautiful. You can see the spirits rise up out of their fucking bodies. That's when I knew that there was an afterlife.

GG: You're morbid. You're fucking morbid.

MS: I'm *not*. I saw the spirits rise. Or maybe it was the hash. (laughs)


TAPE CUTS


GG: You were talking about…

MS: Twenty-three year old boys.

GG: What about them?

MS: They hump mindlessly.

GG: What about 26 year olds?

MS: They're better than 23 year old boys.

GG: Why?

MS: They're a little less mindless. The 23 year old boy was gay though.

GG: I have no idea what you're talking about.

MS: The boy, who drove me crazy until I had to start slicing myself up in his car on the 405. He started screaming like a little bitch. He wouldn't let me drink in his car.

GG: You shouldn't be drinking in his car. You'll get him thrown in jail for that.

MS: Look, I'd suck the cock of a pig before I'd go to jail.

GG: Some of us don't have that privledge.

MS: But I was drinking, not him.

TAPE CUTS

MS: So what they do is...a bunch of rich, West LA little fuckers. They got this big house, that cost about four grand a month, in the Palms area of Los Angeles. They each had their own room. *Their art was all over the house. And they had a stage show in the back yard. There'd be actors and singers and dancers, and they would all skip around the house*!

GG: Why are you talking like that?

MS: Skip da la doo? Skip *da* doo loo? Skip da da lay!

GG: Skip to my *loo*, dear.

MS: Oh yeah. And they would say, "*ooooooooh. Sataaanica!*" I was at their house because I fell for a retarded fag.

GG: What are you doing at night with this fag? In bed, you know.

MS: He was my groupie. I'm doing this show. I hadn't had sex for a while. I was doing a show, and generally, I can get laid after a show. I decided to get laid.

GG: What about getting laid. It must be very easy for you.

MS: Not all the time. You have dry spells, right? People have dry spells. But I was determined to get laid this one night. But I couldn't find anyone to have sex with because all these guys were dorks. It's a fuckin *art show*. Then this one really super-weird guy, who I thought was like a really retarded Russian-I like guys who are kind of retarded. He says, "um, um...Miss Satanica? Um, um, um, may I have...may I *speak* to you?" I went, "whaaaat? Not now." And I ran away. I come back later and he says, "I've been painting you." I'm like, "okay. You're gonna get fucked." (laughs) That line works.

GG: How good was he?

MS: Fucking or painting?

GG: Fuck the painting. How was he in bed?

MS: Pretty good. I took him home and fucked him proper for about two days.

GG: (laughing) Fucked him proper! Hahaha.

MS: Then he started chasing around stalking me. I wouldn't let him see me for about a month. I said, "you can see me on Valentine's Day". I said that I hate Valentine's Day so I'm not responsible. I said, "you have to bring me some vodka." He brought me vodka and a painting with a little homemade card that said "fuck Valentine's Day". That's cute, right? We drank the vodka and went to the Echo Park Film Center. Drank another bottle of vodka. Got thrown out of the Film Center. I went into Taix, the bar you and me went to before. I went in there and screamed to all the old people, "FUCK VALENTINE'S DAY YOU MOTHERFUCKERS!" I started freaking out. Then I didn't remember anything. I woke up in bed five hours later thinking, "ah, no trouble. Thank god!" Because I think I kind of like this guy. I wake up, have a little sex.

GG: Then you find out what really happened.

MS: Like two or three days later. I'm walking down the street in Echo Park and all of a sudden the homies are like "ah hah HAAAH! Bay-bay, crazy mama! You need a sponsor!" I'd been running out in the middle of the street stopping traffic, falling down everywhere. This nice guy I've been telling you about, he tried to help me out and I started screaming, "QUIT GRABBING MY ASS! HE'S TRYING TO MOLEST ME!" I almost got him beat up. "HE HAD HIS HAND ON MY PUSSY!"

GG: (laughing)

MS: But I don't know. I wasn't even there. Then he comes over to my house and he says, "Miss Satanica, I think we should just be friends." I said okay, fine. Friends are great. I started reading him my favorite poem, which is "The Mad Queen" by Eric Crosby. As I am reading "The Mad Queen", he starts freaking out! "I HAVE TO GO!" And then, "I CAN'T LEAVE!" I said, "okay, why not?" "I

46

JUST WANT TO EAT YOUR PUSSY!" "I thought we were going to just be friends." But he can eat my pussy if he wants to…right?

GG: I uh…I don't see why not.

MS: It was the beginning of a long and terrible relationship then went on for nine months.

GG: What if I want to eat your pussy?

MS: Not right now, I'm in the middle of an interview.

GG: Oh yeah, I forgot.

MS: Call my agent.

GG: I don't talk to those pigs. Anyway, I think you are a comic genius.

MS: (affecting the air of a British aristocrat) Oh yes, I aaaam a comic genius. Then I get involved with this idiot who lives in a Real World-type zoom-a-zoom house, and suddenly I am surrounded by-

GG: This isn't the fag?

MS: NO, Gene. Can't you listen? I'll explain how all these fags fit in. Pleasant Gehman is involved in this story too.

GG: She's a fuckin whore.

MS: That CUNT! I'm going to punch her face in!

GG: A whore.

MS: And a cunt and a talantless fuckin hack. For the record. In your fuckin book.

GG: I agree with you.

MS: She's nobody and nothing. She's been trying to be somebody for thirty fuckin years. And you know what? She *still* can't sell more than a thousand books. So anyway, Anthony-

GG: My ear's bleeding.

MS: It *is* bleeding! What happened? Oh you picked something. You're a picker.

GG: I have a habit of scratching my earlobes when I get nervous.

MS: Do I make you nervous?

GG: No, you make me very, very calm.

MS: I'm dating the fag. He's driving me to drink.

GG: *Have* we been driven? Obviously. Because it is not very easy to become a full time alcoholic. Why work at something that is unpleasant if you are not being pushed to do it by people and places that are terrible?

MS: Exactly. I'm on a red wine binge. And we all know what that's like. That's a half assed binge. A real binge is whiskey. Or vodka.
GG: Oh.
MS: We have an act together. I sing and firedance, while he plays piano. He was a great piano player, his only redeeming quality.
GG: I thought you said he was okay in bed.
MS: Well, only twice. We'd be getting down, and he would say, "I think we need to get a prophylactic."
GG: HAHAHAHHAHA!
MS: I'm like, "why don't you just stick your cock in my ass and shut the fuck *up*?"
GG: That's like saying "penis".
MS: "Can I insert my penis into your vagina?" He says to me, "We'll write songs together and sing them…together."
GG: (laughing)
MS: I write a couple songs, right? And of course they're genius. They're the fuckin greatest songs ever. Songs about eating babies. Very catchy. It drives people crazy, actually.
GG: I don't like babies, actually.
MS: You're an easy score, then, you sweet baby. I say, "okay, now let's make some money." The fuckin Velvet Hammer cunts won't let me do anything with fire. I called them cunts right to their faces. Michelle Carr is gonna get a big fat fuckin pie in the face, too.
GG: Who is Michelle Carr?
MS: She's the humorless fuckin cunt that runs the Velvet Cunt and is gonna get a big cunt pie in her cunt face.
GG: Hahahahha!
MS: And you can cunt me on that!
GG: I'll CUNT you on that!
MS: (laughs) I go in there to do this audition, and I'm going to sing this song about eating babies. I think I'm all cute. But I didn't realize when I went that…well, I walk in and there's Pleasant Gehman, and fuckin Michelle Carr, and Rita deCuntberg.
GG: deCunt-*who*? Rita de fucking Cunt-*who*?
MS: Rita Talberg?
GG: I thought you said Cuntberg, but I wasn't sure.
MS: Whatever. Rita Dumb Cunt. Don't print that stuff about that pie. I don't want them to see it coming. Don't blow my pie thing.

GG: I would never cunt you like that.

MS: Yeah man, don't cunt me up! So I walk in and Pleasant and those cunts are all sitting pretty in a row. I'm like, "oh my god, I'm having a flashback to junior high cheerleading tryouts." I had this bottle of prop wine. So I said, fuck these cunts, I'm drinkin the wine. So I'm going GLUG GLUG GLUG, and there's Pleasant going "ehhhhh!" She's saying, "leave me alone!" GLUG GLUG GLUG. The little boy-

GG: The fag?

MS: -was terrified. I threw the corkscrew across the room screaming, "THIS SUCKS!" I did my little song and spilled wine all over their hardwood floors. Then I ripped my clothes off, just sat down on the ground and smoked a cigarette, drank the wine, instead of doing the audition. And they hired the boy instead! After the audition, he said (whispering), "I can't speak to you anymore. It's oh-oh-oh-over. Thank you for everything you've done for me, but I think you might have taught me *too much*!" He's very dramatic.

GG: Why would you want to be with a guy like that in the first place?

MS: Guess who he's with now?

GG: Who?

MS: Vaginal Crème Davis and Ron Athey. They adopted my little boy! And now, he's their *BITCH*! Now he's in all the gay magazines with them. They outed him! They called him Satan's Swish! They gave him a SWISH!

GG: Ron Athey is the coolest there is. And Vaginal saved me from certain doom one night, when I got lost in Hollywood, or wherever the fuck it was. I was so upset, I saw her and leaped up into her arms. She held me.

MS: I think Vaginal is a good woman, and I think she's taking good care of my boy. He had some Greek fantasies so now I think he should take some big fat nigger cock up the ass. And like it. Lord knows *I did*. Hah hah hah hah!

GG: The interview is over.


TAPE CUTS

GG: No, let's keep going. Are you right handed or left handed?

MS: I am ambidexterous.

GG: How did that happen?

MS: I did it as a circus trick.

GG: Why?

MS: So I could tour Europe, and get this trick town.

GG: What is this trick?

MS: To write four different words with my hands and my feet, at the same time. Right now I can write two different words with my right hand and my left hand at the same time.

GG: How long did it take you to learn how to do that?

MS: A few hours a day for a couple of weeks.

GG: What other kind of tricks do you do?

MS: I am learning stilts right now. I can bounce things on my chin. I can do contortions. Fire.

GG: What are you going to do at Dante's on Tuesday?

MS: I'm thinking of doing a Chinese dinner scene. Where I become a geisha, with a parasol, using two minutes of Chinese music I got from Jerry Lewis' *The Geisha Boy*. I am going to sit down and have a little bit of chopstick fire, out of a bowl. I'll strip. Dance around with my torches and do tricks.

GG: What would you like to eat today?

MS: Anything but fire.

GG: What is your band called?

MS: Der Trinken Karnikle.

GG: What does that mean?

MS: The drunken rabbit.

GG: And that night you performed as Der Trinken Karnikle, what did that dirty rabbit do?

MS: He caused a lot of trouble. But the band we opened for really loved us, because they said that we were the best opening act they'd seen on their whole tour.

GG: Why did you want to do a band?

MS: Because I was challenged. Because they wouldn't let me do fire in the Troubador, and I can't be a one trick pony. My friend said, "do *something*, you're a performer, come up with something." He's my mentor, he's *been* my mentor for over ten years. So I can do whatever I want at the Troubador.

GG: Except for fire.

MS: Yeah. So I decided to do something way more damaging. (laughing)

GG: How many people were in the band?

MS: DJ Prickle, and-

GG: (chuckling)

MS: -he is way better looking as a girl than as a guy. He bought all of Lydia's dresses at the garage sale. Now she *loves* him. Prickle was the Green Fairy, and our ballika player. Ballika is a Russian guitar. He really stole the show during the band's hallucination scene. Chirstopher Wonder, the drunk and untalented magician. An old carny style magician. Very handsome and beautiful man. And then there's-wow Gene you smell good.

GG: Yeah?

MS: Uh huh.

GG: That's my natural scent.

MS: You smell like baby powder. And he come out three times in between songs. He hypnotizes chickens by blowing cigarette smoke in their faces. He also shoots rats out of a cannon.

GG: These are live rats?

MS: Uh huh.

GG: Who is the Absinthe Fairy?

MS: That's Prickles. It's Absinthe Cabaret In the Round.

GG: Oh. (laughing)

MS: Chistopher's girlfriend, Clarice the Fire Darling, she can't do fire either. He made dress disappear, by pulling the needles out of her dress, making it go away, and then he pulled the needles out of his mouth, 20 needles, with an invisible piece of string.

GG: That's fuckin insane.

MS: Then we have Chelsea Rasmansan, on cello. She teaches at a music school. She is the cello player for REM and also the girl that the miracle man throws knives at when she's in the circus. She's circus folk too. Mandy is my second piano player to leave the band. The first one being Anthony.

GG: Why did Anthony leave?

MS: Because he's GAY! He didn't want to do my band anymore. He wanted to do the Velvet Hammer. How fucking gay is *that*?

GG: Those dirty Velvet Cunts.

51

MS: That makes their cunts sound good. I should call them the Sandpaper Cunts. Velvet makes it sound like fucking their cunts would be good. Velvet is nice, and they are cunts. Mandy played piano and accordian at the same time. Then there is the rabbit. Rich Polysorbate.

GG: I have been waiting all this time to hear about the rabbit. Please tell me about him.

MS: The rabbit was our chaos, along with Prickle. I didn't tell the girls that there would be chaos there, because they are hardcore musicians.

GG: They're professionals, because you have REM's organ grinder.

MS: Their cello player, Gene.

GG: Oh. But they want a well oiled gig. A real gig.

MS: Right. Me and the girls sat there for weeks and weeks and composed all of our songs together, on piano and cello. It was a very interesting process. I was bellowing. I said, "I am scared to sing!" They said, "you're singing!" So we're all basically tight, but I wouldn't let them meet the drummer. The drummer was going to improv. He's a magician's drummer.

GG: But what about the rabbit?

MS: Oh, the rabbit! He plays drums.

GG: How big is this rabbit?

MS: He's probably about five foot seven.

GG: That's a really big rabbit.

MS: It's a guy in a rabbit suit. The motherfucker wouldn't keep his fuckin mask on, so half of my job that night, between singing, was putting the mask back on his face while he's playing drums, because then he can't stop me. That goddamn rabbit. He is such a handful. Anyway, I didn't tell anyone what was going on and-

GG: Is this a plushy-type thing? Or is it just a guy in a rabbit suit?

MS: It's just a guy in a rabbit suit.

GG: Is he a plushy?

MS: Maybe. He *is* pretty fuckin weird. He's just happy to be in a band with a bunch of hot chicks. Otherwise I have him under control.

GG: Didn't you tell me that the rabbit beat up the band members?

MS: Yeah, because he's into chaos. You have to see his act. It's his band, really. It's named after him.

GG: Which gives him cart blanc.

MS: *Yeah*! It gives him TOTAL cart blanc. We had the kind of crowd where there *had* to be chaos in the band, it couldn't just be good music. It had to be insanity. The chaos people were instructed to keep it quiet. *I* wanted to have a good time, too. I didn't want to be bored! I told Prickle and the rabbit, do whatever the fuck you want to. Cause chaos. And then, I don't know anything. While our very serious piano player was playing piano, the Rabbit put a giant, crazy skull on a fishing rod, on a piece of string, and started bashing her in the head with it.

GG: HAHAHAHAHA!

MS: And it was the funniest thing I ever fuckin saw. She was *so* mad, she was trying to just play. The Rabbit originally wanted to wear an Osama bin Laden mask, and I said, "no Osama bin Laden in this band!" So I don't know *what* he had on at this point.

GG: But that wouldn't work anyway...because he's the Rabbit.

MS: He's the Rabbit. At this point he had duct taped the rabbit head *on* to the Rabbit, because he kept taking it off. He was also trying to get out of his suit. I had to beat him a little bit that day. Anyway, she tried to take being hit in the head for a while, then she stood up, grabbed the skull, and just started smashing it on the floor, in the middle of the performance, which I thought was great! She didn't understand that that was one of the high points of the night. Everyone was laughing at it, but she just got mad and quit the band.

GG: You had band members leaving the band before, during, and after the set.

MS: Yeah. The cello player tried to quit *before* the set.

GG: Because of the Rabbit?

MS: No. This is because of the bullshit people at the Troubador who were fucking up her soundcheck. Also, it was raining out, and cello players don't like the rain. It makes their cellos sound different. Mandy tried to quit *during* the performance. Prickle was fired and re-hired before the performance.

GG: How was the performance received?

MS: The LA Weekly wouldn't cover such a thing. The LA Weekly is nothing more than Pleasant and all of her friends writing about all their stupid things they did last week, or what they're going to do next week. People don't ever write about anything outside their own

53

circle. One critic said that it was the strangest thing that he had ever seen. The strange leading to the strange. He said that "they had a lead singer who bellowed." Well...I *am* a vocal stylist, not a *bellower*, but whatever. He said it was the most remarkable thing he'd ever seen, and a night never to be repeated." I wasn't going to do the band anymore, but then I read that review and decided to keep going. I had a nervous breakdown after the show. For a month, I couldn't even go outside. I was like, "what did we just do?" It really took it out of me.

GG: Are there any other socially revolutionary or socially confrontational things happening in Los Angeles or Hollywood right now?

MS: Well, there's *me*! I'm just trying to help! (giggles) Nobody is. Just me. But that's because I was raised with really good punk rock roots. What I am doing is definitely cabaret. They're very sweet songs, you heard them. But they definitely have punk rock tendencies.

GG: If you ever need a second Rabbit, I'm your guy.

MS: Well, you'd definitely be good chaos. (laughs)

GG: I need your favorite quote, or one of them, to end the interview with.

MS: "Art is crime, crime is art, don't get caught, that's bad art."

GG: This is going to be "The Portland Eight Mile", by Gene Gregorits, with Miss Satanica. The interview is over.

MS: Miss Satanica, Secondary Queen of the Underground...

GG: Because we all know who the fucking first one is.

MS: HAHAHA! YEAH! You should go back to her, Gene.

GG: I thought I just said the interview was over?

# JANUARY 31, 2002

Robert, cab driver

GG: I really fucked it all up.
Robert: Don't worry, everything's gonna be fine. Oh, here we are,
looks like it's closed.
GG: Will you drive me to the library?
R: Sure


TAPE CUTS

   Mere hours after being dumped on the fucking streets, I sober up,
and exit a soup kitchen. I stumble along the street, crying publically,
not caring. I need taken in, looking for a place to drink. I meet
Bobby and his friend, a braindead crack whore, sitting at a bar I
have wandered into. We have a few rounds. I'm buying. I offer to
buy a piece of Bobby's costume jewelery, a silver rope-chain, which
is ghetto fabulous, in exchange for an interview. He agrees. The
crack whore's eyes lights up every time I look at her, so I pet her
hair and smile. Bobby, the crack whore, and I board a bus, the driver
staring at us all with great apprehension. We ask someone how to
get to Radio Shack. The three of us storm Radio Shack, causing a
disturbance but for some reason the staff is amused and eager to
help. I buy a microphone and batteries. We then must stop at Rite
Aid for a disposable camera. When Bobby and I return with the
camera, the crack whore has vanished.
   He is willing to trust me, I assume, because of the scars on my
face. We walk to a nudie bar, and switch on the tape.

APPX. 12 NOON
(All Live Nude)

55

BOBBY: I describe how it looks to me. It may not look like that to the next person, because I have too many problems with the next person. Me and the next person have *never* seen eye to eye.

GG: But you understand what I was saying though?

B: Of course I understand you.

GG: Why are you even willing to talk to me?

B: I wanted to talk to you because an interview is an experience that I have never indulged in before, in my lifetime. It's just an experience for me. I'd like to know how it feels. I'd like to see the outcome of it. It's a roll of the dice. Suppose somebody gets ahold of this and likes it. Or they go and they read it and they don't like it. Still a roll of the dice.

GG: I'm going to give her a dollar. I'm going to give her *five* dollars.

B: No man, you crazy? Give her one.

TAPE CUTS

GG: Would you mind saying hello?

NUDE STRIPPER: Hello.

GG: Wow.

TAPE CUTS

GG: Where did you grow up?

B: South Central Los Angeles.

GG: You mentioned the Hell's Angels.

B: I'm into them because I know a lot of them, a lot of red and white. I get along better with them I've found, in my later years, than I do with my own people. There are people who think I'm lying…

GG: The Hell's Angels are racists. You also mentioned getting along with Klansmen.

B: I say it like that but I mean it like this: any man that looks me square in the eye and goes straight to the bottom line, and push the line like he's supposed to…and not give me no bullshit, I *love that*. That is the best understanding that two men could ever have.

GG: He still hates you for very ignorant reasons.

B: Every man is entitled to his own opinion. If he wants to spend his time living in the dark end of the world, that's him. As long as it don't infringe upon me, and my rights, upon my security and *my* peace of mind, he can do whatever he wants.

GG: Seems like too often, it takes the black man to be the better man in a lot of situations, in an argument.

B: I never consider it the better man in an argument. I feel like *too much* argument is a load that I shouldn't carry. I don't wanna oscillate back and forth. I wanna modulate in the smoothest way possible, that I can. That means getting along with everybody, and kickin it with everybody, regardless of what they feel like deep down inside. You're not supposed to let that show *anyway*. You keep that to yourself, that's your own personal idiosyncracies. I don't look in the mirror with a closet full of skeletons.

GG: You're a beautiful person. Hey look, she's taking off her panties!

B: *Ohhh*, man!

GG: Check that out. What do ya think?

B: What do I think? Why, I'd go up in there quick as I could draw my ass back. Oh yeah. She is fine.

GG: That's the most beautiful woman I've ever seen.

B: You spilled your batteries.

GG: Fuck it, don't need'em. Already loaded.

B: She's not the *most* beautiful. She is very beautiful, but now, understand *this*. Let me re-iterate. Oregon has the most beautiful women in the country. They pick the models from here.

GG: Don't think I'm being rude if I look away while you're talking.

B: And don't mind if *I* look away. Because I can *do* two things at one time.

GG: Me too! And I am, right now.

B: *Ha ha.*

GG: I just threw her five. I can't afford that.

B: Well, I'd have thrown her five if I didn't have only five left.

GG: Well, I'm buying the beer tonight. Well, today! What time is it?

B: Quite early. 12:30, 1 P.M.?

GG: What about crystal meth?

B: My opinion of drugs and shit like that? I feel like this. A lot of shit is supposed to be on the down and low. Only a fool would just put his business out there in the public. There's things that the public just don't understand. The public is confused. Some of them may like what I do. Some of them may *not* like what I do. Some may want to persecute me and prosecute me for what I do. Others? They *pay it no mind.*

GG: How many years did you do?

B: A total of 33.

GG: Your last stretch was for killing someone, and also for shooting a police officer.

B: (pauses) Yeah. Yeah, I did. I killed the one man, and I wounded a police officer.

GG: What about prior convictions?

B: One conviction was under the Lynching Act, when I took my buddy, who was a prisoner of the *po*lice, and I took him out to my car, with a gun. They charged me under the Lynching Act. One incident was a robbery. Another was assault on a police officer. At the time I was out on the Sunset Strip, with a bottle of whiskey, packin a gun. Someone saw it and they called the sheriff. The sheriff showed up and I was so loaded I didn't even know that I had the gun out. It was tucked in my waistband. Friedman suit. You know, I'm sharp. This is how we used to dress in the old days. You know how those OGs dress now? The tennis shoe generation? We did not feel comfortable in tennis shoes, with our pants sagging down. We had been through that with the khakis. I'm losing my train of thought here.

GG: Me too.


TAPE CUTS


B: This gonna sound strange to you homey, but I haven't loved in so long, I been through so much in these prisons, that I *lust.* I lust, I don't love. I feel less than a man if I have to love, unless the woman is contributing deeply.

GG: Being honest, you mean?

B: Gene, check this out. Women is gonna be women. I don't give a damn if she-

GG: How do you know a good one?

B: *All of them* are good. They just gon' do what they do, and you gon' do what you do. You gon'go thirty years in the same marriage? Fuckin the same woman? Your wife? NO. So when she do it? Don't trip. If she smart, she'll do it when you don't *know*.
GG: So you don't believe in there being the "right girl". I guess you think that's all nonsense.
B: Look. All women are beautiful, within their own right. If one is not beautiful in one respect, than another will be beautiful in that respect. But you have to look down deep, to see that beauty in some women, sometimes. But they are *all* the same woman. They're gonna do what women do. How you gonna stop the nature of a woman? It's like trying to fight against the natural laws *of* nature. That's why there's so many babies buried in the monastaries, with the monks and the nuns. That's them trying to fight against that natural law. They go and do their do, and they have to cover it up.

TAPE CUTS

B: Why don't we just try to catch them at a time when they horny?

TAPE CUTS

GG: I'd rather not deal with that. I'd rather just make it up. Lie.
B: That's you're program. If that's what you wanna do, do it. If it's making your world turn, then it's a tool that you need to use. Do your thing, like I said.
GG: Shot of whiskey?
B: No, I can't drink hard alcohol.
GG: Me neither.

TAPE CUTS

GG: All men have masochistic tendencies. Any man who goes to a bar and watch naked women while torturing his liver with booze is a masochist.
B: Well, I don't know about other men, but for me, sex under the influence is the toughest thing I ever went up against.
GG: No it ain't.

B: Then again, women should be a man's *hobby*. Not his muthafuckin *life*. Not his livelihood. Not his fuckin leaning post. They should be his *hobby*.

GG: The world puts you in a position, I think, where you are forced to perceive women as dangerous.

B: The world don't put me in shit. I do what I wanna do. Bitch can be with me if she wanna be with me, if she don't wanna be with me, then *break wide*. That's all I can say. Myself? If I see a shady bitch, and she's fine, and I wanna fuck her, I'm gonna scheme to fuck her. But after I fuck her, I'm goin. If I have fallen in love, then I'm gon'fuck her again. But then I'm gon'fuck her till I fall *out of love*. If I see one I wanna settle down with? It don't make any difference what the bitch is. She could be a hooker. In fact, I would *prefer* a hooker, for the simple reason that a hooker is not going to be enticed by a pretty car, or a nice house, by a diamond ring. Hookers done *had* all that shit. They done *rolled* in Rollses and Benzes. They done had that shit, you know, and ten foot anaconda dicks. So when a hooker love a square motherfucker, she *really* in love with him, from her *heart*. She's not looking for *nothing* that he can give her.

GG: That's a tough scene. I don't think I could deal with a hooker. I'm too petty. I'm into that sugar and spice crap.

B: Then what you need to do, is get yourself another world, next to Wayne's World. Get yourself another one, next to his.

GG: You're saying that I have cooked up some fantastical scenario that could never happen in this life?

B: I'm sayin, basically that it's never gonna happen. I hate to say that. But then again it would make me feel kinda small to say that what you're sayin is not real. You do have *some* women like that.

GG: But they're nowhere! (laughing)

B: You see that, huh? See, I can't stand no bitch that just wants to fuck only me.

GG: Heh, heh, heh.

B: A bitch that wants to do nothing but wait for me to get home. Bitch, you better go get a boyfriend.

GG: You do realize that we are both insane? Look at that! Four feet away. If we were sane, we would ignore the law, and jump up on that fucking stage and get as good a feel as we could before the cops showed up. We are perverting our natural urges, because the law is perverted. It says that women can be naked four feet from us, but unless we're stinking rich, we can't fuck them. I think that's sick. We're crazy people.

B: What? You talkin about touchin the bitch? I would rather run up there and lick the crack of her ass.

GG: Then why not bury your tongue deep *in* her ass*hole*? I mean, while you're down there, why fuck around? Kind of a waste of time, otherwise.

B: See man? I KNEW you was a muthafuckin *freak*! I knew it would come out sooner or later. (laughing) Because it all comes out in the dark, don't it?

GG: (laughs) It does, man. So what happens to you when you do meth? I'm an ex-coke freak myself, so I'm curious. You turn into a sexual demon, right?

B: I see that little funky ass cocaine runnin through people, drivin their asses fuckin *crazy*, and there's no tellin what they puttin in that shit. Listen, the thing about muthafuckin *speed* is-

GG: I gotta switch the tape over.


TAPE CUT

GG: Ziggy played guitar. Go on.

B: Sorry about spillin that beer man, but you just buyin way too much beer at *one time*! I mean, this whole *table* is filled with beer.

GG: That's how I do it. I'm insecure. I like to have plenty around. Look, if I can have a table full of beer, and $40 left at the same time, I'll think about where I'm sleeping *later*.

B: Look man, this forty bucks thing? I don't believe it for one second.

GG: It *is*, man! I was in a fucking soup kitchen all morning. They knew I needed help. And now I'm here.

B: Well, if it is true, then I suspect that you gotta be one hustlin motherfucker.

GG: I have to be. Who the fuck would ever give *me* a credit card?

B: But you don't have to hustle. I can tell, you have a fuckin brain, and a good one homey. You have a very, very high IQ.

GG: I wouldn't know anything about that.

B: Well, maybe not, but when it come to scrappin for it, you gonna have yours. You gonna get yours one way or another. You play on a

61

higher level than I do. I'm what they call a dusty hustler. I ain't no big ol'hustlin motherfucker. I pick up twos and fews.

GG: HAHAHA!

B: I may pick me up a hundred or two a day, that's all. Because I'm a pussy.

GG: That puts you one hell of a lot further ahead than me.

B: I'll get my party material, whatever that is. It's done easy. That's it. But with *you*? I look at you, youngster. Look here. This muthafuckin world *is yours*. All you got to do is bloom like the muthafuckin flower you supposed to be.

GG: That was given to me as some kinda password this morning.

B: What?

GG: That word you just said. "Bloom."

B: Well isn't that somethin. Co-incidental? Probably. Maybe it's in the makins. Maybe you gotta bloom. Right now, I can see that you are torn between two worlds. You could be one vicious, *savage* motherfucker if you would just *let them bitches alone.* Don't try to be right to no bitch, be yourself. And if a bitch like you for yourself, then that's where you be.

GG: Women think I'm crazy.

B: Most motherfuckers I know is crazy. Every bitch I know is crazy. Evidentally, if you tryin to be up there in the wrong circle, and you are not mainting a level of happy medium, then let that shit alone. Johnny Cochran can't function as a motherfucker. If he tried to function below his level, as a traffic court lawyer, *he'd starve to death.* Maybe you just functioning below your level. I can tell, you like this gangster shit out here.

GG: Well, you can call it gangster, it just seems more honest to me.

B: Well, that's what gangsters are. We are true to ourselves. We true to what we believe in. I'm not sayin, "show no allegiance to the next son of a bitch." That's your fellow man. Your fellow man, you treat him with common courtesy. *You* my fellow man. We sittin here *breakin bread* together. Just because that motherfucker over there, at that next table, just because he black, he's not my fellow man. I'm true to my game. If the money fall out of his pocket, and I can get his wallet, I'll get it. Like I say, I'm a dusty hustler. And if you get stupid, I'm gonna get *you* one day.

GG: If I got stupid, I'd deserve it. I have it comin to me as it is.

62

B: If folks can see that you are acting not in accord with yourself, and that you is doing foolish things, then that would be the parting shot. I would break wide. But as long as your cap is on, and you thinkin proper like you thinkin, let shit alone. Let it blow. Because *man*, when I first saw you? I looked and I said, well, this guy right here, he sharp. You know why I said you were sharp?

GG: *WHY*? (laughs)

B: Because you came with *gifts*, muthafucka.

GG: (laughs)

B: Gifts that didn't mean nuthin to you, but gifts that would win muthafuckas OVER.

GG: What gifts? I don't remember giving any gifts.

B: *Ohhh*, man. You gave money. Cigarettes. Beer. To *strangers*, you didn't even know. You took'em out. And what you did was, you established a foundation. And once you established that foundation, you bound yourself to us sayin that you could walk it. And I believe that givin the right situation, if it wasn't a nigga like me? You'd end up *runnin shit*. But now, of course, I'm gonna let you run shit too. Because I'm gonna let you make the money also.

GG: What money?

B: Any money you can.

GG: There ain't no way you could possibly think I'll get penny one for this interview.

B: No.

GG: No. Exactly. *No*. But that's because the (laughing) general *public* does not appreciate quality.

B: What I'm sayin is, you could go out there and get some drunk bitch to *like* you. And wanna give you her lane. You done made *that* money.

GG: I always fuck it up with women. But so what? This interview is turning into something all about me, now.

B: No, it's not about you. Let's say it's about me. I'm not the one with the hangups. Either I'm gonna go to church…or I'm *not*, man. It's as simple as that. If he treat me any other way than as a thief in the night, I'm gonna try and cheat him. That's just how I am. But I'm not a *dirty* motherfucker. There's loyalty among *thieves*. There's loyalty among us gangsters. There's things that we won't do. Period. Some of the things we won't do, we won't do because we have that

63

respect. Some of the things we won't do, we won't do because we fear that this motherfucker is gonna put a bullet in our heads. Black people is like that. White people ain't like that. Y'all just jump up on one another and beat each other up with some horseshoes or some shit.

GG: HAHAHAHA!

B: We don't do that. We plot, we lay and scheme. Maybe that's why I don't get along with my own kind a lot. Because we some *spiteful* muthafuckas!

GG: (still laughing)

B: We can hold grudges for like *twenty years*. It's like, nigga, HOLD UP! Can't you see this is fifteen years ago? Let that shit alone. But we don't have that kinda sense!

GG: You're fuckin crazy, man! You're outta your fuckin mind! HAHAHAHA!

B: No, you LOOK. I am *not* out of my mind. I'm just puttin the hard line down. If I *really* told the truth-

GG: The Red Sea would part.

B: -muthafuckas just wouldn't want to hear it. It'd just remind them of themselves. You understand me?

GG: (laughing)

B: You *understand me*, you jackfoot, nig hip, pot smokin muthafucka? Who thought you was my *friend*? You sucka. I been lookin at your wife and shit, tryin to steal her jewelery, tryin to get into your bank account. *Everything*, you understand me? You white dudes all be together, and when y'all don't like each other, y'all just smash each other with a *fist*, upside the head or somethin. And that's the way it goes. But black people, we somethin else. We don't do it like that. Me? I live in Portland, and I'm out here in the streets, right? *Because I love these muthafuckin streets.* My daddy was a streetrunner. You know what? When my brother-before he died, Eroll Jr.-I was-hey, that fuckin thing on?

GG: No, you want me to leave this part out?

B: No man, leave the shit on. I just didn't see that red light on there?

GG: It aint working, apparently.

B: It *was* workin!

GG: It just came back on. We got all this, don't worry.

64

B: You see, I said I wasn't used to it, but you done used some more of your trickeration on me. You turned it around where I couldn't see it.
GG: I'm kinda funny like that.

TAPE CUTS

GG: I'm in the bathroom alone. I'm gonna read what's in here on the wall of the bathroom. It says "Extenders". We have a selection of fine rubbers. First on the menu is "Slo-Boy". Then, oh here's a doozy. The "multi-extender ring." Hey come on in, don't mind me. Third is, "Midnight Stalker." Thrill her with fingers of passion! Try all six in rotation!

TAPE CUTS

GG: 21$^{st}$ Century Boy. Bolan sucks.
B: I came in because I wanted to see you destroy the tape.
GG: I would not do that because it's a great-NO, WAIT! We need pictures, man!
B: Let me think about that for a minute, my friend.

TAPE CUTS

B: The police done ran my black ass outta California.
GG: I got run out too.
B: And here you are in Oregon. You got me on this tape here. Not that I'm afraid or anything. But it would be foolish for me to stick my head in the lion's mouth. But you can have some pictures, because *I don't give a fuck.*
GG: Neither do I, so let's get some goddamn fuckin pictures already! I'll cross out your eyes. Do I have your verbal, spoken permission?
B: Yeah, you do.
GG: Sir, would you mind getting a shot of me with this gentleman?
SIR: No, I don't mind.
BAROWNER: No. NO. You can not have a camera in here.
GG: Because of the girls?

BAROWNER: That's right. Because of the girls.

GG: I didn't take any yet.

BAROWNER: I'll get one for you.

TAPE CUTS

B: So what I'm gonna do-since *you* say you just arrived here? I'm gonna show you a few things that you can do to come up with some cheese.

GG: Well, I need some *cheese*.

B: Yeah. Then you can get your ass a job, and then you could be my rich friend. But I would rather not see you scufflin *out here*.

GG: I'd rather not be scuffling. I'd get fucked up, I aint street smart enough.

B: I don't want to see you be doin it. Because I want to be able to show you how to manipulate and stack away your money. *Without drugs.*

GG: I don't do drugs.

B: No. Without doin'em, dealin'em, or bein around'em. It's all about what you tell the muthafucka, and it's all about how you present yourself.

GG: What's your last name?

B: Dell----.

GG: That's funny, because my mother has the same four first letters.

B: Well, maybe you my brother, with the other father.

GG: That could be. My long lost brother.

B: I bet your father has money, doesn't he?

GG: No, as a matter of fact, he doesn't.

B: What's he do?

GG: Manual labor.

B: I'm gonna save my last comment.

GG: No, let's hear it.

B: No I ain't gonna say it.

GG: Ya think that girl over there would let me buy her a drink?

B: No, hold back, I wanna say something. See that muthafucka over there? The old dude in them shitty clothes? That's a fine white bitch he got there. What do these women see in these old men without money?

66

GG: Weariness. These old, wise, tired guys. Women love them. Their heart goes out to those guys, just like we like to pick up stray dogs. But I don't know, that's probably full of shit. I don't even like dogs. But no, I think that the best women try very hard to fix men.

B: One thing women don't seem to understand, when their man tell'em, when they look in the mirror, that the only thing that they can see is their ass. They always lookin at they ass, to see if it round enough, firm enough, if it saggin, or whatever. They don't understand that…a marriage is made in the bed. You can tell me if you want, that "oh, I love her because she's so intelligent, and her brain." This bitch is ugly as a lizard. Look here partner. If the pussy ain't good, in the bed? It's a wrap.

GG: That's the sad truth, ain't it?

B: That ain't sad.

GG: Sure it is. It's reality. Reality is sad.

B: No, reality is sad to us because we don't get it.

GG: We're not evolved.

B: Maybe we ain't supposed to be. And you know what one part of that reality is? When one muthafucka can just wake up and see one day that there ain't no such thing *as love*. That poundin in the heart? That deep breathin? Them butterflies in your stomach? All that came *from your stupidity*. There's *super-stupid, colossal stupid, and gigantic stupid*. Me? I'm just stupid.

GG: I guess you're right. Why else would we be sitting in a bar at one in the afternoon?

B: What you want me to do? Try to go do some construction work somewhere? And feel like I am being responsible to myself, and the world, at eight dollars an hour? Shit, I'd rather be out here. Where everything is *soft*. Where everything is under *my* control.

GG: But it's so cold. It's wet, and rainy, and lonely.

B: Well…there wasn't no cowboys that figured like that when they came to America. The scared stayed. The weak died on the way. And the strong made it. I *like* that shit. This is my life.

GG: A beautiful woman dances naked behind us. They are playing "Where Is My Mind" by the Pixies, on the sound system. As it fades out, so will we. Thank you Bobby.

B: You're welcome.

GG: The interview is over.

TAPE CUTS

APPX. 2 P.M.
Terry, patron

(Note: Tom Waits is blaring, and how fucking appropriate)
TERRY: There's a lot of nude bars in Portland.
GG: Yeah? But what's the best one?
TERRY: Well, that is an extremely difficult question. There are over 53 nude clubs in Portland. And 250 magazines.
GG: You don't think you are torturing yourself, as a man, looking at a naked woman?
T: I'd like to run them. I'd like to run the goddamn club.
GG: Why?
T: Money.
GG: What about the girls?
T: Yeah sure…*they're pretty*.
GG: (cackling)
T: Are you from the New York scene?
GG: Yes. I write for Details.
T: So you're gonna run one?
GG: They don't pay me for stories. I owe them $16,000 for my drug bills.
T: So what are you going to do with the girls?
GG: I will try to tolerate their total mockery of me, like the rest of us. What do they have to do with anything, at this point?
T: Huh?

TAPE CUTS

I show up at Dante's to meet with Miss Satanica, and take in her spectacular fire performance. She is under the impression that I have never been interested in her work, because during my two and a half years in Los Angeles, I didn't make it to even one of her gigs. But I *was* interested, only busy, creating Sex & Guts 4 with Lydia Lunch. I want to apologize to her. I'm wearing a new pair of glasses, purchased for me by my mother several days ago in Harrisburg. ("I

68

want you to have these because your eyes are the only thing you have not yet managed to destroy.")

I like the world better blurry, but I'm wearing them anyway, so as to look more professional, and offset the healed gash which runs lengthwise down my right cheek. It's my best scar, but I have some obscure desire to make a good first impression with Dante's bartender, an unspeakably attractive blonde rock'n'roller whose band, The Balls, interests me greatly. It is tragic that I can't remember her name.

DANTE'S
appx. 9 P.M.
Unknown, BALLS VOCALIST
GG: You're into the whole self-deprecation thing?
Unknown: Talking badly about myself?
GG: Yeah.
U: Only for manipulative purposes.
GG: What's your band called?
U: We're the Balls.
GG: That is the best band name in the world.
U: Why, thank you.
GG: Could you recommend a good local brew?
U: Sure.

TAPE CUTS

Siren, Suicide Girl

GG: You're with Suicide Girls, aren't you?
SIREN: Yes!
GG: I'm a big fan.
S: Really?
GG: Yeah. But I have to say though, that I don't think your boss Spooky is too happy with me. I published an IM conversation with her. She blew me off. But I was being a jerk.
S: Oh, I'm sure she's forgiven you.
GG: Can I interview you for Sex & Guts?
S: For what?

I stalk and stomp around the club, talking to girls, because I am under the delusion that tonight, unlike any other night, I have charm. Satanica's performances are incredible, and there a few very talented strippers before and after her.

I get a hard-on.

I go home with Satanica.

# JANUARY 30, 2003

I wake up late after a night of drinking. Having promised Corrine to be on that fucking plane, no matter what, I run like mad to catch a bus to the Greyhound station. Board the 9:14 to Philly without a second to spare and hop out in Philadelphia. During the cab ride to the airport I begin shaking. I'm elated. I'm saved. Everything will flow easy and beautiful. I'll stay locked in her room with her, we'll bask in countless records, films, bottles of red wine. We won't even *think* about getting dressed for a minimum of 48 hours. I have a smirk on my face you'd need a crowbar to wipe off.

Obsessed, smitten, a love-bug junkie on a thrill ride with all guarantees in place. I am not counting on a whiskey episode, nor on myself to be in another dead mood wherein I could see everything, and know everything, know I am behaving horribly, yet do nothing to stop any of it.

Too much to forget, too many hours, too many dreams, too many fantasies of kissing, too much wanting in out of the miserable fucking Pennsylvania cold, too much destitution, too much invested, too much ingested.

Pennsylvania scams. Pennsylvania binges.

Hocked piles of books and movies. Pre-sold magazines.

Hocked and pre-sold everything.

The only way to live, waiting for her phone call. Waiting for her postcard.

Nightmares of crashing airplanes and Corrine thinking I have bad breath at the airport even if the plane makes it.

But having no choice.

Take the money and run.

Run to Portland, and don't look back.

# AFTERWORD

## Gene Gregorits

The term is derived from a long, long road in Detroit, which is the first major barrier bewteen the suburbs and the ghettos. As you venture further south, you hit seven mile, six mile, five mile. The scenery darkens. The landscapes worsen. Eventually you will arrive in the heart of the city, which, while subject to many attempts at revitalization, remains one of the harshest urban centers in this wonderful country of ours.

The Eight Mile is a sociopathic cattle-car trip straight into the heart of ultimate darkness, which can be plotted and played out in any city, although it works especially well in its eponymous home turf. I deployed my first Eight Mile in Portland, Oregon. Things did not go well. But the point of an Eight Mile is to willingly ALLOW things to not go well. The point of an Eight Mile is self-subjugation. An Eight Mile is a continuous, increasingly rancid, and painful throwing of oneself to the wolves, for at least seven days. One's emergence is met by a strange euphoria, and a heightened sense of compassion, not only for oneself, but for the individuals one does not normally encounter, unless homeless, destroyed by enormous circumstantial tragedy, or, of course, in the depths of a vicious, angry Eight Mile.

An Eight Mile requires the following predispositions:


Chronic depression
Failed relationships
Addiction
Anti-social personality disorder
Talent


PART ONE: The Seduction
Bottom out with drugs, alcohol, and use also a recently condemned marriage as your springboard for psychotic self loathing and hunger for abject failure. Quit your job. Squander your savings in bars, openly attempting to fornicate with ANYTHING THAT MOVES. When not drinking in bars, hard-wire yourself to your computer, melt into the numbness of Internet junkie free-fall. Seek out the woman with a pretty face and a snotty attitude. A woman with no money, artistic ability, drug problems, drink problems, and an axe to grind. Seduce the woman with hard-bitten poetry and prose morbidly fascinated with the irreconciably masochistic response one has to the brutality of life in the modrn age, how it exists everywhere, how it afflicts us all, and especially, how it is murdering you piecemeal-style. Latch on to her affectionate voice during 3 AM telephone conversations. Preferably, the girl you find would live at least 400 miles away, in a major US city, one which you are in no way familiar.

Drink a minimum of 25 cheap beers a day, preferably cans of Milwaukee's Best. Surrender your soul to toxic delierium, night sweats, shaking hands. Stomp out at least two love letters a day. Stay on top of the romance, do not let a single 24 hour period pass without a phone call, an e-mailed love poem, or an unnecessary apology. Sell off as many of your most cherished possessions as possible, to raise the cash for round-trip airfare. Buy also a cheap briefcase, so as to appear professional and driven. Fill it with items that enhance this superficially implied importance, such as reporter notebooks, books of philosophy, the Old Testament, a tape recorder, and a microphone. During your Eight Mile, it is absolutely imperative to be driven by an assumed professionalism. It is also imperative to be IMPAIRED. Bring with you, even if you scraped up a larger amount, no more than $75 American dollars.

Then, GO.

PART TWO: Flight

Drink heavily the night before your departure, thus inflaming your already cheap-yeast contorted cranium with delusions of good luck because you are the last passenger to board the plane. Drink heavily on the plane, using the excuse that it is flight-anxiety. This need not be a REAL excuse; if you are naturally vertiginous, your conscience is clean and you may drink with even greater fury than the non-vertiginous man. However, you must NOT terrorize the flight attendants. Your behavior on the airplane must be extremely well-considered, for a mid-air outburst would place you not in the arms of your long-distance sex and love receptacle, but the local authorities. Your Eight Mile would already be blown to smithereens. Focus instead on the idea of the thirty-ton vessel in which you sit, consuming whiskey and beer, being blown to smithereens. Fear will keep you straight, until it is time to begin your alcoholic zig-zag.

PART THREE: The Strange New World

De-board the plane with delusions of salvation, and, if possible, an erection. Swagger down the aisle loudly, unintentionally striking the other passengers with your briefcase, and then into the greeting area, where the woman waits with a similarly ecstatic vibe. Your first kiss should occur public, at the airport. It is also reccomended that you squeeze her buttocks indiscreetly.

Let the woman reccomend the bar as an ideal location for your first engaging conversation. Drink anything and everything she places before you. Flirt with the bar maid, as best as you are able, and let there be no question as to your actual level of intoxication. Soak up the glory that is the presense of a beautiful woman in a bar, who loves you.

## PART FOUR: Consumation

At the woman's place of residence, you permit yourself to be unable to act appropriately. You march naked through her home while dancing badly. The woman may herself have had to much to drink. If this is the case, do not remind yourself that you are far, far worse. When she becomes unconscious, do not join her. Continue along in what can only be described as a relentless mission to empty her home of all alcohol beverages The next morning, she will awake to find you still going strong. You will have, at this point in the week's festivities, realized that your shame and humiliation are far too great to allow for a teary make-up session, and certainly no making out. Your only sanctuary is to be found in more and more bottles. Allow the woman, upon having reached her limit, and after threatening to phone the police, to extricate you from the premisis.

## PART FIVE: Stranded.

You may walk the streets of the strange city with a feeling in your stomach that is emotionally like nothing else imaginable, and physically like taking a kick from an enraged and over-worked horse (the effects of the cheap yeast and whiskey will only enhance this sensation), but you must also not lose awareness of your dilemma, for the damage done to your wallet by the previous night's drinking should have left you with no more than forty dollars.

You weep publically, leveled by your huge loss, leveled like a building destroyed by depth charges. But you march on because there is nothing else you can do. This fright and panic will only encourge, and may even expand your naturally poor ability to speak to strangers. Having lost your unicorn, and annihilated what little pride remains in you, you are in a mild state of shock, and combined with the geographic disorientation, leads to a nervous jag of extreme cheerfulness.

When no one is looking, punch yourself in the nose as hard as possible seven or eight times, or until bloody. Upon your arrival at the city's soup kitchen, despite your briefcase, you will be appraised as a damaged man, which of course you are. On the way to the soup kitchen, purchase as many beers as can be forced into the biefcase. Be sure to observe the poetic strangeness of the beer cans along side the notebooks, literature, and tape recorder. This vision is sure to instill in you a sense of natural born gonzo, you will slide into fantasies of being Hunter S. Thompson. This exaggerated myth, and heightened sense of self, shall emblazon your social graces. You shall then be well-equipped to handle the pressure of lying openly to anyone and everyone, about who you are and why you are here.

## PART SIX: Using the streets

The early day air hits you like a shot of something strange, and you will respond to this with awe. You will have an epiphianic moment, or a series of them, and with the blood dry on your lips and mouth, begin a full scale assault upon the general public and it is O-KAY, because you are traveling now in God's channel. You will seek out criminals and degenerates, swapping what remains of your money for their time. In bars, you will consume their life history. You will inform your subjects that you are a reporter for Rolling Stone Magazine, new to the job but ON the job nonetheless. You will click open your briefcase in full view of the recently-released murderer or the drug fiend, so that they may take in the edifying spectacle of your reporter notebooks, your tape machine, and your bible. The bible will stand out, invite questions. You will activate your tape machine and let those questions lead further and ever deeper into the darkest recesses of the human soul. Your subject will know those recesses well. He may be blunt, or poetic (poetic, for your imaginary editor, is better, but you are a genius and may poeticize freely at a later date.) Later, you will grow tired of thugs, and you will have been seperated from your last American dollar. You will beg rough women for sex, turning on true charm. Your psychosis will expand your pupils, your eyes will appear to be solid black, creating an intoxicating sex vibe. These women will see you, a microphone wire stretching to your shirt or coat pocket (a coat works best, therefore it is best to conduct an Eight Mile in a cold place,

during the winter season) and they will see the microphone in your hand. You will be the embodiment of pure charm, innocent loneliness, because you have no choice. You have a return plane ticket that is dated five days from now, but your survival during this interim is your problem. From there, you are on your own.
(2005)

**The following excerpts are from the forthcoming novel *INTRA-COASTAL: ONE YEAR ON ST. PETE BEACH*, by Gene Gregorits.**

# LAST EXIT TO ST. PETERSBURG

Detective Tim Fontaine, Baltimore P.D., and another detective, a humorless middle-aged female, are staring at me over a metal table with handcuff rings built into it. I am not handcuffed. I have not been arrested. I am cooperating with the police.

For the last three weeks, Detective Fontaine has been investigating me about a knifing incident that I have sworn to them took place in a dark alley just off the 400 block of Lanvale, which I remembered as the location of the shooting of Kima Gregs in the eleventh episode of The Wire's first season.

The truth is that I slashed my own arm open several miles north in Roland Park, with a serrated edge J.A. Henckel's "EverEdge" steak knife - purchased at Macy's in a set of 13 blades that same summer- because my girlfriend was standing in front of the television and refused to move. I'd been trying to watch Ken Burns' documentary about prohibition, the girl was laughing at me, and I had reacted quite badly to her mockery. I nearly bled to death into a black Hefty garbage bag during the ride to the emergency room. I received nearly 50 stitches, in three layers, while flirting aggressively with the nurses                                      there.

The female cop began speaking, during a very impersonal three minutes of the pair making notes on yellow legal pads and looking at me as if I were a streak of feces on the wall. Finally the woman spoke:

"Mr. Gregorits, I am Detective Royer. We need to put this thing to bed now.

Detective Fontaine's got real cases to work, and hopefully, we can clear this matter up today before it wastes any more of our time. We're not accusing you of anything, but once a report is filed, we are obligated to investigate. That's how it works, and you have just opened a *huge* can of worms. Do you understand that?"

"You think I am making this up? Look, I have a flight booked to Florida. I've had an extremely rough couple of years, and I just want to get out of Baltimore and start over. I don't care if you find the guys that attacked me or not. It was just some punk kids!"

"We understand your situation, but we've reviewed all of your statements, and they're just not consistent with the account given to us by Tess Riordan. Nothing adds up here. Anyone who sat and looked at my notes would think you were protecting someone. You can't explain how you contacted Tess after the attack. You can't provide a description of your assailants. After 7 P.M. on, you can't really account for                anything                concrete.                "
"Look. We'd both been drinking. I already explained that I was actually blacked out during much of this. I'm a blackout drunk. I lose large chunks of memory when I drink like I was drinking that night. I remember being attacked on Lanvale, and I remember walking to The Charles Theater to see my co-workers prior to that-"

"Which is why you were in the area, you've said, but Miss Riordan claims that you were with her, at Jerry's Belvedere, all the way up on Old York Road, and-"
"I was there earlier, but she was watching football, and I hate football, so I left, and started drinking. I went to the movies with two bottles of wine, and-"
"You said you saw the movie at 5:15, and you said you had the stub."
"I still have the stub, yeah. Anyway-"
"What was the movie?"

"Drive, with Ryan Gosling. I also had bought a sandwich, a gyro, at the Greek place across the street, that I had for dinner at the movie."

"And then you walked down to North Avenue and wound up on Lanvale."

"I don't even remember the end of the movie. But yeah, I might have taken a bus, but I know I didn't take a cab because I never take cabs, they're expensive."

"In the time frame you've given me here, you couldn't have walked. Vicky, see if you can pull the tapes from that night's 32 bus. So you went back to The Charles. And why again did you go there, to see another movie?"

"No. Again, I worked there for a few years, and I am friends with some of the employees still. I always stop in and say hello."

"Tess made mention that you were also drinking in another bar in Belvedere Square, Swaller At The Holler."

"That must have been a different day. I don't remember going there at all."

"How did you contact Tess from the Lanvale area?"

"I must have asked someone on the street for help. I don't remember."

"We'd check her phone but she claims to have lost it, so we really can't verify anything now.

"Tess is a drunk. She loses her phone all the time."

"Have you considered not drinking so much?"

"I'm working on it."

The detectives sighed and craned their necks and looked at each other. They didn't believe a word of it.

I'd been in this situation many times before, but this was the first time that they suspected the female of knifing me. My great fear that night was a stint in the mental hospital, for there is nothing that terrifies me more than captivity. I've been locked up forty or fifty times in my life, and it never gets easier. Fear of incarceration was such that I had willed from myself an impeccably controlled performance, and an explanation for the two and a half inch wound that was sufficient for the doctors, if not for the police. As a concession to political correctness, I never actually identified my fictional attackers as African American, but my moral considerations stopped there.

My great fear on the afternoon of August 27th, during that six hour sweating in Baltimore Street's grimy precinct house, was that Tess would go to jail, and that her brother Rick, a Baltimore homicide cop, would have the charges dropped and come after me.


A week later, another ex of mine persuaded me to see her, using a night of drinking in Fell's Point as bait. Carly seduced me in a men's room, and I woke up many hours later, a few blocks from Lanvale, with my ribs broken, my skull cracked open, and a badly sprained ankle. My wallet was gone, and so was my Army pack, which had been full of books, a computer, and fresh donuts from the Lexington Market. The donuts bothered me most of all.

I wondered if it was the cops who beat me up, tired of my mind games. Tess may have mentioned it to her brother. North Avenue was dangerous, so it may have been a legitimate street mugging. If that's the case, the incident appears karmic in nature. It doesn't matter now.

My flight was booked for Monday, September 5th, 2011. Without I.D., of course, I'd never be permitted to board the plane.

So Tess drove me to Pennsylvania, where a DMV clerk listened to my sob story and granted me a new photo license.

The next day, Tess drove me and Sam to Baltimore International. Sam's carrier was deemed unacceptable for travel. I remembered that Tess had been drunk when she purchased the thing at a Towson, Maryland Wal-Mart, and had a traffic accident on the way home.

There was a surge of wet, leaden guilt:

Poor Tess.
Poor Sam.

A young woman at the Delta ticket counter found me another carrier for $50. The purchase left me with only 15 and change. But lives can begin anew with fifteen and change.

Mine did.

On St. Pete Beach.

# FUGITIVES

The rank humidity I encountered in the access corridor of Tampa International airport enveloped me like a fecal sauna. The three hour flight had unsettled Sam, and I was eager to set him free from his plastic carrier. I half-ran directly to baggage claim, and retrieved my duct-taped sack of clothing.

As I turned around toward the exit doors, I found my welcoming party standing there: Tim's sleazeball leather wristbands and Tim's gauche tribal tattoos, Tim's rotten teeth, Tim's greasy grey hair, Tim's acne scars, and Tim's freakishly large belly. Tim had never worked a day in his life, and he was the most horrific caricature of "burnout" that I had ever seen.

We embraced and pretended to be friends. He wore a salt and pepper goatee which announced him, or so he believed, as an artistic man, but rather pronounced his exceptional Hispanic ugliness. It served only to lengthen and sharpen his already long and grotesquely pointed chin.

"Are you shitfaced?" he smirked.

Before I could even respond, before I'd spoken a single word to him in Florida, I already wanted to tear his throat out: standing there with him, in the middle of Tampa fucking International, was Jax, his cowardly and unaltered 10 year old mutt. Sam, already traumatized from the flight, hissed and trembled inside his comfortless carrier.

Feigning obliviousness, or ignorance insofar as Sam was concerned, the homely creep had actually stooped this low to assert his feeble dominance: he'd brought his fucking dog. I had never explicitly asked him to leave the thing at home, assuming that Tim possessed at least that much common sense. I should have known; it was to the very first in an endless series of cowardly and cringingly desperate power maneuvers on Tim's part; exactly the type of behavior that defined the man, behavior which I now understood had only gotten worse over time.

\*\*\*

Tim Ramirez considered himself a landmark underground publisher, having bungled his way through the layout design and public release of an undiscerning arts and culture journal called "Esoteric Babies". There had been several issues. He

88

blackmailed family members for booze money and had manipulated several friends back west into springing for his super-premium "Bali Shag" cigarette tobacco, and similarly top-shelf organic dogfood for Jax, who he had always encouraged to defecate as freely as possible on neighbor's lawns, in broad daylight. He spoke only in a faggoty and conceited whisper that no one ever wanted to hear; it was blasted by too many years of sloth and fear and dope.

Tim Ramirez was the most treacherous, most toxic man I'd ever met, a dangerously jealous and helpless man; it was those qualities, and the depth to which he was both aware of them and imprisoned by them, that made him dangerous. He'd latched onto me after a chance meeting in a Los Angeles bar that I had zero recollection of. Being a man who specialized in bartering with the goods of others, it didn't take much to arouse his interest: cash, a car, a drug connection, a literary association, or even a bar tab. In my case, it was a famous girlfriend. I had a tendency to spout off about her at that time; we were splitting up and I wanted everyone to know that. Tim would size up a man's holdings almost as if by osmosis, and immediately the beady eyed sociopath would begin organizing the transfer of the material, or the information he had verified. You'd invite Tim over for drinks, and by the next day, you'd be neck-deep in a deal with man you'd never heard of, under terms you didn't remember agreeing to; a deal which benefited only your new pal Tim Ramirez. Mr. Moocho Rising.

Over the years, I'd always kept him at arm's length, ignoring his constant suggestions that I move out west to share an apartment with him in Chico, CA. It was obvious to me from the very beginning that Jim was mortally petrified of work. He had been honing his sociopathic instincts, and avoiding common sacrifices for so long that his serial mooching had become nearly effortless to him. And much to the horror of his victims, Tim -as with any genuine mooch- was completely shameless. Tim's face itself had shifted over the years: the sloth and the flimsy excuses and the lying had given him a sleepy appearance. He was "over-underworked." His eyes drooped and betrayed blatantly in them was a nauseating look of guilt, but Tim's sleepy, guilty eyes were both of them thoroughly manufactured things, for he got plenty of sleep (Tim was strictly nocturnal, so as not to get in the way of the working people around him) and the false shame, worn for so many years to incite pity, had simply taken over: a permanent "mooch mug". In ten years, I knew better than to mention work to Tim. If you made even the slightest implication of moochery to him, Sensitive Whispering Tim would shatter and explode right where he sat (or, in a rare moment, where he stood) and be replaced by Violent Humiliated Tim.

As woundingly obscene as it was to witness Violent Humiliated Tim Ramirez, this side of him did -if only fleetingly- earn the implications of his ridiculous forearm tattoos and leather wristbands, which otherwise, much like his deliberate and determined flatulence, only highlighted a crazed urgency to mask his multifaceted impotence in any masculine facade available to him, such as philosophical banter.

Tim proclaimed himself relentlessly to all within earshot to be a philosopher, prizing only the weakest or loneliest individuals from the world around him; these people he would try to establish as his constituency...druggy old dwarves, hirsute barmaids, sleazy lawyers, petty crooks, and failed musicians like Tim himself.

No genuine literary sort would willingly break bread with the fraudulent cretin, and I was no exception. In Detroit, in Baltimore, for years and years, I ignored Tim's 3 and 4 and 5 A.M. phone calls, which he made at a disturbing regularity despite my pleas to him.

Me: "Tim, I have to work."

Tim: "What do you know about work? I work!"

Me: "You do not work, Tim. You have never worked."

Tim: "Fuck you motherfucker! You can't even drive a car!"

Tim's pickup truck which had been given to him by someone, and he believed that this also was proof of his virility.

Tim fancied brotherly ribbing to be a sign of exalted machismo, so he indulged in it frequently, but it was to remain very one sided. You could not get personal with Sleepy Hungry Ashamed Lonely Tim. In dealing with him, I regarded him very much as a menstruating schizophrenic woman on speed: kid gloves, in other words. That's what Tim demanded of all those around him.

"Geeeeeeene,", he would begin, while sucking on a joint stoically, "you don't understaaaaaaaaand....I went to HAR-verrrrrrrd, and I'm a phi-LOS-o-pherrrrrr, Geeeeeene....I'm not going to wash DISH-es like youuuuuu, Geeeeeene, I'm not like youuuuuuu...and I have a HER-niaaaaaah, Geeeeene, I have HEALTH problems.... You should try to learrrrrrn from me, I could make you a better WRI-derrrrr, Geeeene....you're not egreeeeeeee-gious, Gene, but you're just not graaaaaaaaa-cious...."

***

I was appalled and furious, doing my best to contain myself as Tim's dog —which was nearly as big as me- repeatedly broke wind in my face and bruised my testicles with its paws while trying to walk in a circle inside the truck's cab. Sam recoiled in misery below, between my ankles, as we began the 45 minute drive from Tampa International to St. Pete.

In its idiotic enthusiasm, the shaggy gray and black dog smacked me in the face over 20 times with its tail, and Tim continued to say nothing about it, while brazenly powering the grotesquely oversized pickup truck over the Tampa Bay highway. "Jax", he would mutter, absently, intentionally failing to influence the dog's vile behavior. I ground my teeth and moaned in rage as Tim briefed me on the night's agendas. Finally, as he was handrolling one of his Bali Shag cigarettes, steering with his knees in a self-conscious attempt to look cool, I had to say something to him:

"God DAMMIT! Look, I just had a really rough flight with Sam, and Sam is not doing well either, flying is very hard on cats, would you PLEASE? The dog?"

"Jax!" This time he was audible to the subnormal beast, and it retreated into the narrow space behind the driver's seat, panting and groaning like a hypersexual mongoloid.

The bay was several miles wide, engulfing us: I recalled this stretch of road from my wasted bus trip all those years ago. I started hoping that the shock of all that dark water would remain as exciting to me.

With the mutt momentarily keeping its snout and stabbing paws out of the general area of my dick, Sam leapt to my lap, out of his carrier, and stood on his hind legs, bracing himself against the glass of the driver's side window with his paws. He began licking his lips and furrowing his brow, deeply unhappy with the whole situation.

I was desperate to calm my nerves with the first drink of the night, and to get Sam sorted out at the house. I was delirious when we arrived. All shadows, strange smells, someone's home. I hadn't had a proper home in 3 or 4 years.

The house had a massive American flag installed at half-mast above the low front stoop. It was a blue, two story affair, quite pleasant, really, if middle class excess is really your bag; well-furnished but noticeably unclean, quite sickeningly so, with large dust motes and clumps of sticky dog hair co-mingling along the grimy baseboards. Tim, altogether devoid of irony, stated to me at that exact moment: "Geeeeeeene, it was part of an agreement between me and Johhhhhn that I have to clean the houuuuuuuse, so don't make any fucking messsssssses, okaaaaay? You've got to help me cleeeeeeean."

An expensive leather sofa dominated the living room along with a high end digital stereo receiver, a plasma TV, a small redwood bar which was obliterated by layers of dust. The bottles were all empty.

My first impression, even in my debilitated state, was that a lot of effort had gone to presenting an image of swank bachelorhood, a kind of Details Magazine cool,

We made our way to the bar.

# ROUTINE ONE

Sam was soon spending his days lounging in the red tanbark which comprised the whole of John's front yard, with ferns and several flowering bushes. Each day I woke to that feeling one had as a child when summer hits, the shock of a new routine, a new kindness...the giddiness of hot breezes and that kid-frenzy released by chlorinated water and hot sun and and lemonade and murmurings of parents and relatives who would always be there, and of course the freedom of weightlessness. I knew that in my obscene tropical paradise there would be old worries and old agonies for a short while longer, but even these would be filtered through a new lens, a sun bleached "none of this is real" lens, and Sam had all the lizards in the world for his own yellow eyes to chase.

I would find myself walking from 8th Avenue down to Central, the tawdry and synthetic main drag, the division between north and south St Pete, exploring the rancid alleyways and the posh Tampa Bay waterfront, hellbent on finding work. I completed nearly a hundred applications, dismally and angrily. Chinese take-out food was a distant memory, a symbol of better times. I was lucky to have eggs and potatoes back in John's kitchen.

Men's Health Magazine had just ranked St. Pete as "the saddest city in America", and Creative Loafing, the region's sterilized and lobotomized alternative weekly paper, was fairly up in arms about the designation. Apparently, this finding had been based on the city's skyrocketing suicide and mental illness rates, and during my explorations, I observed an overwhelming contextualization of the Men's Health claim: the tropical urban squalor was epic in scale. I began to resign myself to it all. My new home was a frightening mixture of pulverizing poverty, of aggressive spiritual heaviness, of physical degradation, of weather beaten inertia.

Half of downtown's buildings seemed to be flophouses, where the befouled bodies of scourged men could be seen lounging in the stagnant afternoons, chain smoking their one dollar packs of "little cigars". I later learned that these ersatz smokes were comprised of only 50% tobacco. The other 50% was -is- unknown, but from the looks of St. Pete's walking wounded, it wasn't fit for human consumption. Ancient air conditions gone crimson with rust sat in the 2nd, 3rd, 4th, 5th story windows of flophouses staining the gruesome old buildings' cinderblock and stucco walls with dark waterstains that smelled of body odor and nicotine and death. There were dirty yellow awnings that had been painted decades ago with names like The Seville, or The Dalton, or The Tropical Arms. The lopsided and sinking palatial library, situated on Mirror Lake, became a regular destination for me. I would drag myself in there after a day of filling out job applications, eager for the body shock of air conditioning, and cold water. Bums were sleeping in its various alcoves and on all the benches. The library stunk of shit and booze. But it was quiet. Next door sat the Social Services building where hordes of poor blacks and and whites would congregate, chain smoking out front, lining up in the various offices for free food, free money, or free housing. I applied for food stamps there and while I turned my back to pick up my army bag, a black war veteran standing in line behind me snatched my ten dollar cellphone off the clerk's counter. He stared at me defiantly, pink keloid scars roaming from his nose down to his chin.

The sad, dreamy Mirror Lake area was a haven for vagrants and drug addicts of all sizes, shapes, and colors. Stretching a solid mile and a half around, you couldn't deny the beauty of the lake itself, and I would spend the odd hour there pretending to be homeless and rapping with hustlers, fantasizing about cool shady bars, and crack whore sex, and Chinese lunch buffets, and anything else a penniless man imagines for himself.

For the first time in so long I was in a position to allow myself a free-range kind of personal investment, a concentrated interaction with my surroundings; I'd been seeing the same things over and over again, the same places, the only real difference being the physical disintegration of acquaintances...the gradual liberation of memories over time, memories that I never wanted in the first place.

Here in Florida, it was if I had woken up on another planet, a place that was detached in every way from all other places, and its specialness was reaffirmed everywhere I looked; in my periphery, always, whether passing through a sandy vacant lot, down an alley, through the open air drug market known as Williams Park, were lizards of a startling variety: Mediterranean geckos, tropical house geckos, brown anoles, green anoles, knight anoles, racerunners...billions of omnipresent beasts ranging in size from 3 to 12 inches, and on a bright 95 degree day, I would walk for hours just to enjoy the sight of them darting across sunbaked shelves of sidewalk, with a stealth and agility that made me feel like Bobo the Dancing Bear. Before inevitably spooking a lizard into shelter, it was impossible not to stop and stare, contemplating them and their disconcerting spasms and tics, with a little brown anole's head and most of its body alternating between two different frozen poises, back and forth, like a strange little machine, short-circuiting there without any sound at all.

100

ingramcontent.com/pod-product-compliance
ing Source LLC
bersburg PA
V021152090426
0CB00008B/1055